WHY YOUR PARENTS ARE HUNG-UP ON YOUR PHONE AND WHAT TO DO ABOUT IT

PENGUIN BOOKS

UK | USA | Canada | Ireland | Australia
India | New Zealand | South Africa

Penguin Books is part of the Penguin Random House group of companies
whose addresses can be found at global.penguinrandomhouse.com.

www.penguin.co.uk
www.puffin.co.uk
www.ladybird.co.uk

Penguin
Random House
UK

First published 2024

001

Text copyright © Dean Burnett, 2024
Illustrations copyright © Katie Abey, 2024

The moral right of the author and illustrator has been asserted

Text design by Mandy Norman
Set in Amasis MT Std 11pt/17pt
Printed in Great Britain by Clays Ltd, Elcograf S.p.A.

The authorized representative in the EEA is Penguin Random House Ireland,
Morrison Chambers, 32 Nassau Street, Dublin D02 YH68

A CIP catalogue record for this book is available from the British Library

ISBN: 978–0–241–67959–3

All correspondence to
Puffin Books
Penguin Random House Children's
One Embassy Gardens, 8 Viaduct Gardens, London SW11 7BW

MIX
Paper | Supporting
responsible forestry
FSC® C018179

Penguin Random House is committed to a
sustainable future for our business, our readers
and our planet. This book is made from Forest
Stewardship Council® certified paper.

DEAN BURNETT

Illustrated by Katie Abey

WHY YOUR PARENTS ARE HUNG-UP ON YOUR PHONE AND WHAT TO DO ABOUT IT

PENGUIN BOOKS

Dedicated to my own children,
Millen and Kavita.

This is what Dad was doing when he
was sat in his writing shed all that time.

CONTENTS

SOME BASICS ABOUT THIS BOOK

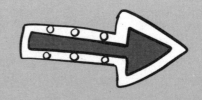

HELLO!

To begin, I'd like to say thanks for buying this book.

Unless . . . you *didn't* buy it. Maybe it was bought for you as a gift from a relative or friend. Or maybe you got it from a library or your school . . . If so, please pass on my thanks to whoever supplied you with this book.

Unless . . . you didn't *want* this book and it's been imposed on you by whoever *did* buy it. I'm not thanking someone who goes around forcing people to read things they don't want to read! Who even *does* that?

You know what? I've confused myself now. So let me start again.

Hello! And thanks for choosing to read this book. I hope you enjoy it.

There, that's better.

SO, WHO AM I, EXACTLY?

I'm Dean.

Dean Burnett, to be precise.

Doctor Dean Burnett, to be even more precise.

For the record, I'm not a *medical* doctor. Don't come to me for help with broken bones, ruptured organs or anything like that. At best, I'll do nothing. At worst, I'll *try* to help, which will end up with you feeling much worse.

No, I'm the other kind of doctor. I'm a scientist. A *neuro*scientist, specifically. I study and know about the brain and nervous system. How they work, what they do, all that stuff. And when you realize that the brain and nervous system are responsible for *everything any human has ever done or experienced,* you come to realize that 'all that stuff' is quite a lot.

However, I've never been into running brain experiments or working in the lab. Instead, I love *talking* about the brain, and eventually this became my actual job. First as a teacher and lecturer about all things mental health and beyond, then as a writer – of articles, columns and, eventually, books.

One of my books was for older children and teens. It was about the differences between their brains and their adult parents' brains, and how these differences explain the constant arguments between parents and older children. I also explained why these arguments aren't automatically the younger person's fault, despite what many adults say.

That book was called *Why Your Parents Are Driving You Up The Wall And What To Do About It*. It was pretty popular. So much so, my publishers said, 'If you ever want to do a sequel, just let us know.'

And I did want to do a sequel.

This is it.

WHAT'S THIS BOOK ABOUT?

Well, it's about . . . the same thing as the previous book. Sort of. But with an important difference. This book focuses on a common cause of arguments between parents and teens.

Basically, this book is about phones.

As in, smartphones.[1]

1. Because smartphones are the type of phone everyone has now and they do all the stuff parents worry about. And it'd be weird to write a book about older phones that people your age hardly ever use any more. I might as well write a book called *Why Your Parents Are Grumpy About Your Gramophone.*

I'll bet any amount of money that you and your parents have had many disagreements about your phone. Perhaps because you *don't* have a phone but feel you need one, except your parents don't agree. Or perhaps you *do* have a phone, but your parents object to how much you use it. Or what you use it for.

Either way, the result is: arguments. Between you and your parents. About phones.

You might have noticed that parents (and other adults) have a whole range of 'concerns', which they talk about during arguments about phones. How many of these have your own parents done?

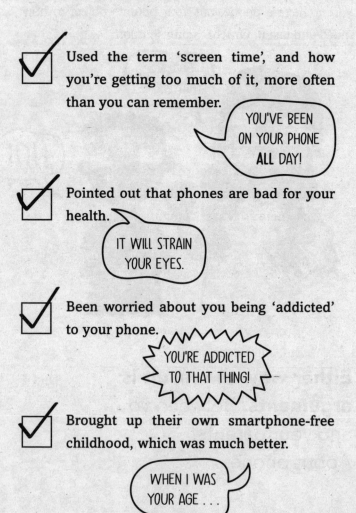

Used the term 'screen time', and how you're getting too much of it, more often than you can remember.

YOU'VE BEEN ON YOUR PHONE **ALL** DAY!

Pointed out that phones are bad for your health.

IT WILL STRAIN YOUR EYES.

Been worried about you being 'addicted' to your phone.

YOU'RE ADDICTED TO THAT THING!

Brought up their own smartphone-free childhood, which was much better.

WHEN I WAS YOUR AGE . . .

✓ Insisted on no phone use at night or before bed because it ruins your sleep.

IT'LL KEEP YOU UP ALL NIGHT!

✓ Accused you of being rude or antisocial because you're always on your phone.

GET OFF YOUR PHONE AND COME AND SAY HELLO TO GRANNY!

✓ Raised concerns that you're talking to too many people, including strangers and suspicious types, via your phone.

CAREFUL WHO YOU'RE TALKING TO.

✓ Not noticed that those last two things contradict each other.

Parents everywhere say these things *all the time!* So it would be surprising if they were all wrong.

The thing is . . . they *are*. Wrong, that is. Mostly.

Nine times out of ten, all these claims about the dangers of phones are *not* based on genuine brain science. Usually, it's the opposite! It's basically an avalanche of wrong information being vomited out into the world and constantly repeated by adults, who really should know better.

So *that's* what this book is about.

The actual facts
about how phones
and devices affect you
(and everyone else,
young or old).

It's also about how you can *use* this information – to separate the things your phones can do to you that your parents are *right* to be worried about, from the worries they have that are more to do with their own paranoia.

Hopefully, by doing this, rather than having yet another argument, you can start a genuinely helpful discussion and reach an agreement with your parents around the subject of phones and technology, and end up with a better understanding of phones and a less stressful life for everyone.

It's worth a shot, right?

WHO ARE YOU?

The sort of reader this book is aimed at is a typical older child or teenager, between 11 and 16 years of age. If that's you, hi! I hope you enjoy what's ahead.

Of course, if you're younger than that, I'm still happy for you to read this book. (Not sure how I'd stop you if I wasn't happy, to be honest.)

Similarly, if you're a parent or other actual adult, you're also welcome to read this. But you might get rather annoyed by what I'll be saying about you. If you are, don't say you weren't warned.

Anyway, I'm going to assume you, the reader, are an 11- to 16-year-old. One who regularly argues with their parents about phones.

Now, here's the thing. There's been so much written about what young people should and shouldn't do with their phones, but most of it ignores one crucial aspect: *actual young people* and what *they* think. Most of the stuff out there about 'the dangers' of phones is basically adults telling other adults what they should be telling their children to do/not do with their phones. What their children think about this is, apparently, unimportant.

Adults who like to moan about phones and 'kids today' seem to think that the second you give a young person a smartphone, they instantly turn into some wretched goblin-type creature, staring at their precious shiny thing in their dank cave, furiously hissing at anyone who tries to take it away.[2]

That's why I'm writing a book aimed at you, not your parents. Young people are often *more* able to grasp the facts about the pros and cons of phones.

2. Gollum, basically. From *The Lord of the Rings*? If you haven't seen *LotR* . . . well, I can't help you.

We'll look at the effects of screen time, the impact of phones and technology on your brains, attention spans and memory, whether or not your parents' phone-free childhood was *actually* better, the risks (and benefits) of connecting with people online and loads more.

After all, your youthful brains are still fresh and can retain new ideas and information. They haven't spent decades absorbing the waffle spewed by adults who think Snapchat is a type of breakfast cereal.

So let's get started!

BEFORE WE GET STARTED

Actually, before we begin properly, I need to clear up a few things to make sure we're all (literally) on the same page.

WHAT DID YOU CALL ME?!!?

I explained earlier that the target reader of this book is 'a young person between 11 and 16 years old'. That's a bit wordy, though. I can't keep saying 'young people between 11 and 16 years old' or this book will end up twice as long as it should be!

Unfortunately, there's no single word that specifically means 'young person between 11 and 16 years old'. At least, not as far as I know. And I write words for a job!

I could use 'child'. It would be *technically* correct. But it lumps you in with nursery-school kids and this book's definitely not for them. Also, it's a bit . . . patronizing? After all, at your age you've probably had more than enough of adults lecturing you about what you should and shouldn't be doing or thinking because you're 'a child'. I will only get on your nerves if I do that too.

So, basically, I'll be using a mix of 'young person' and 'teenager' because those are both technically correct and don't sound weird. But whatever term I use, I am definitely referring to you, my 11- to 16-year-old reader.

I don't want to *exclude* anyone, though.

Most of the things in this book apply **to everyone**.

However, some aspects of technology clearly affect young women more than young men and vice versa. And when you include factors like gender fluidity into it, that makes it more complex again.

So, to make things easier for everyone, I'll try to *include* everyone, in all the things I cover. Except for when that wouldn't make sense. You'll see what I mean soon enough. I hope.

TECHNOBABBLE

I've said this book is about phones, and it is. But it's not *just* about phones. I say phones to mean *smart*phones, but I'm using smartphones here to represent all devices that parents get worked up about. Sure, it could be your smartphone. It could also be your games console (Nintendo Switch, Sony PlayStation or whatever), an iPad or similar tablet, a smart TV, a laptop or anything else along these lines.

Basically, if it has a screen and allows you to access the internet, that's the sort of modern technology I'm talking about. I just say 'phones', as that's, at the moment, the most common example.

Also, I say 'modern technology', but, if I'm lucky, this book will be read by young people for many years to come. And technology changes *quickly*.

So, while the technology I refer to in the book may be recognizable as I'm writing it, if you're reading this in the future, even the very near future, it may not be.

Maybe by the time you read this you'll be able to watch TikTok videos on the soles of your trainers – and your parents will be getting all worked up about the damage young people are doing to their knees by constantly pulling their feet up to their faces. It could happen!

Luckily for me, technology may change quickly, **but the workings of the human brain do not**.

And I doubt teenagers and their parents will suddenly stop arguing in the next ten years. So most of this book should still be useful. Some of the tech terms and references will be out of date, is all.

Also, even if all the technology I talk about is current, it's still *me* talking about it. Me, a man in his 40s, in the 2020s. I'll definitely end up saying stuff that you find hilariously out of date, without even realizing. Sorry about that. Hopefully it'll be funny for you, at least.

PARENTING ISSUES

When I talk about arguments you have with your parents, I may use terms like 'mum' and 'dad'. They're just the most common examples of parents. But it's not the *only* examples. Far from it.

You may have a single mother or father. You may have two mums or two dads. Maybe you're being raised by grandparents or other relatives or foster or adopted parents.

All these are valid. When I say 'parents', I mean 'the adult or adults responsible for raising you'. And if I say 'mum' or 'dad', that's just . . . me being lazy.

One final point, and it's a serious one: while this book is aimed at helping you deal with phone-based arguments with your parents, I'm assuming that the relationship you have with your parents is normal. By 'normal', I mean that they complain about your phone and device use because, ultimately, they *care* about you. As parents should. They mean well; they just have a different take on the matter, one that may be . . . let's say, 'misinformed'. They *mean* well, but they're not always *right*. Which is pretty much the point of this book.

Sadly, not everyone is that lucky. Some young people's relationships with their parents aren't so positive. They may have parents who are excessively controlling, emotionally distant, competitive, toxic or worse. *Much* worse.

There are many reasons for how this could happen. For now, if you are one of the unfortunate young people with parents like that, there are some resources that might be helpful for your situation at the end of the book.

I think that's everything?
So *now* let's get started!

CHAPTER 1

'ARE PHONES BAD FOR YOUR HEALTH?'

'YOU'RE GETTING TOO MUCH SCREEN TIME!'

Let's talk about screens. The flat bit on your phone that lets you use it.

Specifically, let's talk about 'screen time'. Countless parents can get . . . really weird about their kids spending too much time looking at screens. For instance, maybe you're someone whose parents, or grandparents, insist that looking at a screen too long will 'give you square eyes'?

If so, I can relate.

Back in the 1980s, when I was six, I'd watch TV by sitting very close to the screen. Like, *really* close. If a newsreader had had their tonsils removed, I'd have known.

My parents, grandparents and every other adult in my life didn't like this. They'd regularly tell me that sitting so close to the TV would mean I'd 'end up with square eyes'.

Like it was a confirmed medical fact.

Eventually, I went for an eye test, where the optician discovered I was so short-sighted it was a miracle I could see my own feet.[3] That's why I was sitting so close to the TV screen: I genuinely couldn't see it. So I got glasses, could see the TV fine and sat at a normal distance away from then on.

The optician never said anything about my eyes being square, though. Why? Because *that's not a thing*! Seriously, how could a screen *change the shape of my eyeballs*?

---

3. OK, he didn't say those *exact* words. But he could have! I was *really* short-sighted.

In fairness, TV sets in the 1980s were huge brown boxes that weighed as much as a small car. They also produced loads of heat and static electricity and made mysterious noises. Who knows what they had inside them. Gunpowder? Radiation? Infinity Stones? It was anyone's guess.

But still! It's scientifically impossible to have your eyes and bones turned square just by looking at a TV screen. So why did my parents and family keep saying the opposite?

And why am I even telling you this?

Well, it's to show you that parents having a go at their kids for staring at screens isn't a new thing. Despite now being a middle-aged balding adult scientist, part of me will always be that little kid being harassed by his parents for looking at a screen. Even though I wasn't doing anything wrong and their reasons didn't make sense.

If this sounds familiar to you – well, you've come to the right place. So let's look at the actual facts and hard data about screen time.

'WHAT *IS* SCREEN TIME?'

What exactly *is* screen time?

The obvious answer is 'time spent looking at a screen'. So that answers that. On to the next chapter!

'NO, *SERIOUSLY*. WHAT IS SCREEN TIME?'

I *am* being serious. The words 'screen time' include 'screen'. And 'time'. And . . . that's it. Can't think what else it could mean, really.

'OK, FINE. SO WHY ARE OUR PARENTS SO WORRIED ABOUT SCREEN TIME?'

Ah, now that's a good question. But before I answer, let me ask you one in return.

My parents were constantly worrying about me staring at the TV, but that was back when I was a kid. *Your* parents are much more likely to be worried about – you've guessed it – phones!

However, if you have a parent who's strict about your screen time, what do they do if you're looking at a screen that *isn't* the one on your phone? Do they panic? Try and get between you and the screen to stop it corrupting their precious child? Do they destroy the screen with a heavy object, like it's a scorpion that's found its way into their shoe?

Or do they do what every other parent does, which is absolutely nothing?

The thing is, it's pretty much impossible to avoid looking at screens these days. They're *everywhere*! In schools, libraries, shops, on buses, attached to buildings, in cars, in gyms and so on. Parents and other adults are so convinced screens are bad for kids, that they put them up everywhere and on everything, to the point where you can't *not* look at them . . . Sure, that makes sense.

When research showed that breathing in other people's cigarette smoke was bad for young people, the adults in charge banned smoking in many public places. What they *didn't* do was assemble a vast army of smokers and tell them to wander the streets and blow smoke into the face of every child they found. That would be ridiculous.

But that's exactly what's happened with screens. So what's going on?

The simplest explanation is that parents and adults **don't *actually* believe** that simply looking at a screen (any screen) is bad for you.

Have your parents ever said that you've had enough screen time and then told you to do home learning on your laptop or watch TV with them? That's basically them saying, 'You've been looking at a screen for too long. Look at a different screen instead.' And that . . . doesn't make sense.

Your parents might say it's not simply *looking* at a screen that's bad for you, it's the amount of *time* spent doing it. Hence the term 'screen *time*'. It's sort of like sugar:

It's nice to have *some*, but too much, and it quickly becomes bad for you.

That *still* doesn't explain things, though. If, for example, one hour of screen time a day was the safe amount, you could burn through that in a single morning, without a glance at your phone! Purely thanks to all the screens in the world around us.

No, it seems that most parents, whether they recognize it or not, think only the screen on your phone is harmful. Or the one your video-game console is using. Or the TV showing the videos you like. Basically, it seems like the only screens they worry about are the ones you *like* to look at.

What a coincidence!

'OK, SO IS THERE ANY REASON WHY STARING AT A SCREEN FOR TOO LONG COULD BE BAD FOR YOU?'

Now we're getting somewhere.

Usually, when parents tell you stop doing something because it's bad for you, you can at least *understand* their concern, whether you agree with them or not.

If they tell you to stop riding a bike without a helmet, it's because they're worried about you falling off or crashing and injuring your head.

If they tell you to stop drinking Coke or energy drinks, they're worried you'll damage your teeth or be so wired you'll struggle to get to sleep at a sensible hour.

If they tell you to stop juggling venomous spiders, it's because they're worried about you being bitten by a confused, angry, toxic arachnid.[4]

---

4. True, venomous spiders provide *many* things for your parents to worry about. Still, everyone needs a hobby.

But when they tell you to stop looking at screens . . . what are they worried will happen to you, exactly? (And don't say 'square eyes' because we know that's nonsense.)

How can looking at a screen be dangerous or harmful? You're barely even moving when you do it. Nothing on the screen can actually touch you. It's not even really there, technically. Things can't hurt you just by you *looking at them*, after all.

Actually, they can.

'WAIT, THINGS CAN HARM YOU JUST BY LOOKING AT THEM?'

Yes. You can be harmed, or at least affected, just by looking at something.

Take, for instance, a solar eclipse, when the moon briefly blocks out the sun. If you ever got to see an eclipse, you'll have been told repeatedly to *not look directly at it*. You need special glasses or viewers. This is because if the high-energy rays from the sun hit the retina in your eyes for long enough, they can seriously harm them, damaging your eyesight.[5]

Granted, that's the actual sun. Most things you look at aren't million-mile-wide balls of nuclear fire. Can smaller things affect us, just by being looked at?

Yes. Our eyes and vision aren't like the camera in your phone: they don't just record whatever they're pointed at. Vision is the sense your brain relies on most to figure out what's going on in the world.[6] Which means certain things we see can trigger odd reactions in our brains.

'WHAT SORT OF THINGS AFFECT US BY LOOKING AT THEM?'

Well, there are colours. Certain colours trigger certain responses in our brain. Bright red can trigger excitement, fear or alarm, while sky blue or light green

---

5. Technically, you don't need an eclipse. Looking directly at the sun at any time could lead to this. But during an eclipse is usually the only time we can look at the sun for long enough to cause this damage, as most of its brightness is hidden.
6. Unless you're blind or visually impaired. Then other senses take over. The brain is flexible like that.

produces feelings of calm. That's why you rarely ever see bright red in hospitals (unless a surgery has gone *spectacularly* wrong).

That's another thing: if we look at things like car wrecks or open sewers,[7] we can become upset or disgusted. Again, looking at things obviously *can* affect us. It just depends what we're looking at.

They don't even need to be vivid or detailed things. Research suggests that our brains can experience anxiety when we look at . . . triangles.

Simple triangles.

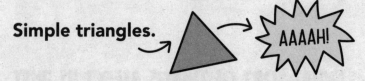

Why? One theory is that our brains evolved over millions of years in the wild, where many of the dangerous things were 'pointy'. The fangs and claws of predators. Jagged rocks. The barbs and stingers of poisonous insects. Thorned plants. All pointy things. And pointy things are *triangular*. So our brain learned to fear triangles. Just to be safe.

7. My primary school once took us on a trip to a sewage treatment plant. It was as much fun as it sounds.

It's not a *big* fear reaction, of course. We don't run screaming at the sight of bunting.

It's more like our brain can go from 20 per cent anxious to 20.05 per cent if we see triangles. It's easily ignored. But it's still an example of your brain being affected by simply looking at something.

'SO SCREENS STRESS OUR BRAINS OUT?'

Well, they *can*. But they can also do the opposite. Calming games and apps, mindfulness stuff, meditation videos, chillout music, getting advice and reassurance from others, even the act of putting everything in your calendar or notes can be calming. All these can occur while you're looking at your phone's screen.

Which means it's not so much about stress. But screens can make your brain *work* harder. Sometimes too hard.

This might sound wrong. Why would watching a video via your phone make your brain work harder than, say, reading a book? After all, both involve staring at a rectangle a few inches from your face. Surely reading a book, a novel, and decoding all the words and concocting all the characters and places within your own imagination is *more* work for the brain? Compared to watching a video, where everything is made for you in advance?

Unfortunately, our brains don't work that way. They have to process everything we perceive, so presenting your brain with *more* stuff means it has more to deal with.

You know when you're with your parents doing a big shop at the supermarket and have to pack it all into bags at the checkout? Your brain looking at things is like that. With a book, it's like getting a slow cashier, sending one item down the conveyer belt every ten seconds – so bagging everything up is easy.

With screens, especially if you're watching something fast and 'busy', it can be like the cashier is rapidly flinging your groceries towards you. Things end up in the wrong bags, the yoghurts have spilt and so on. It's not that your brain *can't* handle it, it's just more work to do so.

And this will affect you. You've probably noticed that you're really tired after a full day in school, even though you mostly just sit there and listen to teachers talking. But even though you aren't moving around much, your brain is dealing with all the information being thrown at you. And, after a while, that can be as tiring as physical exercise. Similarly, things on a screen, even if they're fun, can eventually be exhausting for your brain.

This is backed up by studies, which show that if you have a concussion, reducing screen time means you recover faster.

Think about it: if your brain needs time to recover and reset from a head injury, making it work harder will slow it down. Just like with a sprained ankle, it will take longer to recover, if you insist on jogging every day.

Overall, it's hard to deny that screens make your brain do more work. And that's not always ideal, because your brain is always doing a lot of work anyway, and it only has so much time and energy to spare. Especially if it's injured and trying to recover. If you make it do more work on top of that, it doesn't help.

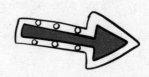

'DOES THIS MEAN OUR PARENTS ARE RIGHT? SCREEN TIME IS BAD FOR US?'

If a parent is sneakily reading this, they're probably punching the air in celebration. After all, I've proved them right.

However, if you are that parent . . . slow down, sunshine.

Some parents may point to studies that show that too much screen time is bad for you – and so believe you should put down your phone – and while such studies do exist, most of them happened *before* smartphones were a thing. It was TV screens they were concerned about, something parents are usually less bothered about nowadays. So, technically, these studies don't say anything about phones being bad for you *at all*.[8]

And even the studies that say screen time is bad for you always include long explanations about how the data is nowhere near as simple as that.

Basically, the reality is much more complicated than 'Phone screens are bad!'

8. And you know what? *Not one* of them mentions anyone getting square eyes!

'SO HOW MUCH SCREEN TIME IS TOO MUCH?'

That's a much harder question than many parents realize.

Yes, looking at screens *can* have unhelpful, even harmful effects on us, like by showing us distressing stuff or slowing down an injured brain's recovery. It makes sense that the longer you spend looking at screens, the more likely these things are to happen. So parents and adults are right to put limits on screen time.

But those same parents aren't bothered when you're looking at screens other than the one on your phone. As I said earlier, that feels a bit . . . convenient.

The truth is far more complex. So much so that obsessing over screen *time* is actually not very helpful. Yes, many people in charge say that a firm limit on screen time is the only way to go. But what do people who've actually studied it say? For instance, the UK's Royal College of Paediatricians (the organization of people responsible for deciding what is or isn't good for young people's health) – what do they say the limit for screen time should be?

Well, they don't. The Royal College of Paediatricians don't advise parents to put firm limits on how much screen time you get.

How screen time affects you is determined more by **how you *react* to it and what is *on* the screen.**

Because screens can show you *anything*. That's basically the point! And you could use your screen to read a book or watch a nature documentary for five hours. Or look at something deeply gory and upsetting for ten minutes. Guess which one will affect you more? In many ways, limiting screen time because it sometimes shows harmful things is like trying to ban shoes because someone's going around kicking people up the bum.

That's not to say unlimited screen time is the way to go.

But when it comes to how screen time affects you, **the most important aspect is . . . *you*.**

How you respond to it, what you choose to do with it and so on.

In a way, the content you choose to consume is, to your brain, like what the food you eat is to your body. Some of it is healthy and good for you, and some of it is junk food and bad for you. But the junk food is often more *enjoyable* so most people prefer to eat that if they have the choice.

But the thing is, parents may *think* that some screens, like the one on your phone, only provide sugar and junk, so try to keep you away from it. But that's just not the case, scientifically.

So if you're going to be talking to your parents about this matter, it's important that you know as much *actual* information about how screens and phones affect you as possible, right?

Good thing you're reading this book, then!

'PHONES ARE BAD FOR YOUR (PHYSICAL) HEALTH!'

I think we can all agree that it's not just you 'looking at a screen' that bothers your parents. It's more that doing this is bad for you. As in, bad for your health.[9] After all, they're your parents: keeping you healthy is a big concern for them. Because they care so much about you.

(Also, if they don't do it, they could go to jail. But mostly it's the caring thing.)

But *how* is looking at your phone bad for your health? After all, you're literally just staying still and staring at a glowing rectangle. Surely that's not bad for you?

---

9. In this section, I mean *physical* health. Your body, your fitness and so on. We'll get to mental health very soon.

Unless, I don't know, a meteor crashed into your living room and vaporized the chair you were sitting in while looking at your phone? But that's just bad luck. You might have been sat there reading a book instead. What would the meteor have done then? Said, 'Sorry, my mistake', before veering off sharply to the left and taking out your neighbour's garden shed? Not likely.

No, common sense says you can't possibly damage your health while using a phone.

But that's the weird thing about common sense: it's not that common. Which is why your parents can be overly worried about the dangers of phones.

And sometimes, their worry leads to weird ideas.

'ARE PHONES BAD FOR YOUR HEALTH?'

If someone insists that phones literally make you sick, ask them this: Where are all the brain tumours?

You may also ask, why would anyone ask such a bizarre and horrible question?

Well, early mobile phones, from the 1990s or early 2000s, were chunky, brick-like things that got really hot and shrieked at you.[10] But the worst thing about early mobile phones was that they gave off radiation. And radiation gives you tumours. So a mobile phone held next to your head for long periods would *give you a brain tumour*!

It's amazing how many parents (actual adults, with jobs and houses), believed this was 100 per cent true.

Luckily for them (and everyone else), it's nonsense.

Actually, that's not fair. Mobile phones do *technically* give off radiation. In the form of radio waves. That's a type of radiation harmless to humans. If you don't believe me, consider this: another form of radiation, even more powerful than radio waves, is light. Never mind mobile phones – light bulbs and lamps should be pretty much *lethal*. And yes, parents never panic about them. Weird.

10. Early ringtones were high-pitched and unpleasant.

But like I said just now, parents often struggle with common sense, so this mobile phone tumour rumour stuck around.[11]

But you don't even need evidence to challenge this fear; you just need to think about it sensibly.

Billions of people now use mobile phones. And if phones *did* cause brain tumours . . . we'd see *billions more brain tumours*, right?

We don't, though. The latest evidence shows they occur no more now – or less – than before mobile phones were invented.

Here's another good question: Why exactly am I telling you this?

When you're told something is dangerous or bad for you, it can be unsettling. Scary. And life has enough anxiety already when you're a young person, without having your parents ranting about how your precious phone is hurting you.

---

11. Also, using your phone while filling your car with fuel is still banned in many petrol stations in case a spark occurs in the phone's electrical innards and ignites the petrol fumes, causing a big **kaboom**. That such a thing has literally never happened and is virtually impossible doesn't seem to matter.

But this whole 'invisible brain tumour' thing really makes clear that it's important to look at the facts and think about things sensibly, before assuming that something is dangerous and telling everyone about it. That leads to rumours, suspicions and pointless panics.

Unfortunately, many people (and parents in particular) can be way too paranoid about the harm phones can do to your health, without good reason, even if they totally believe it.

So, to separate fact from fiction, let's look at the actual science of how phones affect your health.

'SO DO PHONES DAMAGE YOUR HEALTH?'

Not really, no. There are very few ways for a smartphone to directly damage your health.

If someone threw a phone at you hard enough, or dropped it on you from a great height, it could do some serious harm. But . . . that's not the *phone's* fault. Unless 'being a solid object' is a crime now. If you're going to blame anything, blame physics and gravity. And, you know, whichever idiot is throwing or dropping phones.

Also, a phone would directly damage your health if you ate it. All the hard, sharp bits, and the powerful chemicals in the battery would make a right mess of your insides. And that wouldn't be fun for anyone.

However, let's be honest, even the most paranoid parent isn't worried that you'll use your important, expensive phone as a projectile weapon. Or a snack.

Aside from those extreme cases, there's hardly anything a small, slim, smooth rectangle can do to directly harm you.

'HANG ON, WHY DO YOU KEEP SAYING DIRECTLY HARM YOUR HEALTH?'

Ah, well spotted. I say it because *the phone itself* isn't doing anything particularly harmful. It's not blasting you with radiation, it's not covered in poisonous chemicals, it can't reach out and punch you in the face.

But it can harm you via *indirect* means. Maybe it doesn't do anything to you – but the things *you* end up doing because of your phone? They *can* hurt you.

'WAIT, DIDN'T YOU SAY EARLIER THAT SITTING DOWN AND LOOKING AT YOUR PHONE IS TOTALLY SAFE?'

Ah, I did, didn't I? I shouldn't have said that so confidently, because it's not 100 per cent true.

My bad.

Here's the thing: thanks to how it evolved over millions of years, the human body is meant to move. In fact, we can keep moving longer than many other species. Very few animals could even hope to run a marathon, but humans do it for fun![12]

However, this means that, as humans, we need to stay active to keep our bodies healthy. Meanwhile, a 'sedentary lifestyle' (regularly staying still for long

---

12. Apparently, the average horse can run 20 kilometres before needing to rest. That's a *half marathon* for humans . . . although we don't run half marathons with a whole other human on our back, so maybe it's not a fair comparison.

periods) is bad for your health, causing greater risk of diabetes, heart problems and more.[13]

And if you're looking at your phone for hours on end, it means you're pretty much motionless the whole time. And that's very much a sedentary lifestyle.

'DOES THIS MEAN THAT IF WE JUST MOVE OUR BODY MORE WHILE USING OUR PHONES WE'LL BE FINE?'

Not exactly. Just to confuse matters, sometimes phone use makes you move *too much*. Which is also bad.

Repetitive strain injury, RSI, happens when one part of your body regularly does the same thing, over and over. Your body, amazing as it is, still experiences wear and tear. Professional tennis players, with all that jumping around and smashing high-speed balls, regularly suffer from serious elbow, wrist, and knee issues, despite being top athletes in their thirties.

---

13. Of course there are many reasons, physical and mental, why someone may not be able to exercise regularly. There are ways to compensate for this. However, despite what many insist, being healthy does NOT require you to be slim, thin, buff, etc. You can be healthy with a wide range of body types and shapes.

But you can also get RSI from using your phone. It's pretty common. All those hours of scrolling or sending endless Snapchat messages with your thumbs puts serious strain on your fingers, joints, tendons and the nerves in your hands and arms. It can cause numbness and pain that can potentially spread up to the elbow.

So, your phone can mean you don't move your body enough, which is bad for your health. It can also mean you move certain parts of your body too much. Which is also bad for your health.

I did say it was confusing.

'BUT I'M YOUNG. ISN'T YOUR BODY WEARING OUT SOMETHING THAT HAPPENS WHEN YOU'RE OLD?'

Good point. You younger people, you can probably do parkour for 15 hours a day and barely break a sweat. Me, in my forties, I have to be very careful when bending down to tie my shoelaces in case my spine crumbles to dust. However, in some ways, being young works *against* you.

Here's the thing:
bodies change.
Regularly.
And they usually
change in response
to what you do with them.

For example, if you move house to one at the top of a steep hill, you'll suddenly spend much more time than normal climbing up a hill. Because you need to get home.

As a result, your body will go:

WE SEEM TO BE CLIMBING HILLS A LOT LATELY. IT'S HARD WORK. LET'S BULK UP THE LEG MUSCLES SO CLIMBING HILLS IS EASIER.

And so your leg muscles get bigger and stronger. Over time, your body adapts to what you do with it.

But if you spend too long hunched over your phone . . . *that's* what your body will adapt to do. It says:

> HUNCHING OVER A LOT, ARE WE?
> OK, THEN, GUESS ALL THESE BITS WE USE
> WHEN *NOT* HUNCHING AREN'T IMPORTANT,
> SO WE'LL LET THOSE WITHER.

Your body basically learns unhelpful lessons and makes less-than-ideal physical changes, leading to bad posture, poor muscle development and more negative stuff. And these things can cause lasting damage.

This whole 'body changing' process is *particularly* important during your teens. That's when biology says, 'We need to turn this child body into a mature adult one . . . so what do we need to make that happen?' Which means your teenage years are when your body can be *upgraded*, in a sense. It's growing and enhancing anyway, and the things you do with your body during this time will help shape how it does this.

And it's not that you can't change your body as an adult; it's just harder. So if the bodily changes that happened during your teens are *un*helpful ones, they can last quite some time.

'BUT IF WE JUST STAY ACTIVE WHILE USING OUR PHONES, WE SHOULD BE FINE?'

It wouldn't hurt. Technically, a *variety* of movement is most helpful, to avoid RSI at least. Running, jogging, walking, climbing, rowing, bike riding. As long as it's varied and doesn't focus on just a few select bones and muscles, it's all good.

Also, phones can often be *helpful* when it comes to your health. For example, your phone gives you access to countless exercise, diet and training guides or apps. Or maybe you just want to join in with TikTok dance trends. It's all exercise of some sort. It all counts.

Also, one of the main things you use your phone for is to communicate with friends, to arrange to *go somewhere and do something*. Whether it's to play football, go to the shops, arrange days out, whatever.

'ARE YOU SAYING THAT MY PHONE ACTUALLY IMPROVES MY HEALTH?'

They *can*. Many things you do with your phone can make you more active, more aware of your health and so on.

But then, there are things you can do with your phone that are very bad for your health too. Beyond just sitting down too long or straining your thumbs.

If we're out and about, but still constantly looking at our phones, that can be dangerous. Many young people do things like wander into busy roads because they're engrossed in their phones. I've almost hit a few with my car![14]

And it's not just that they can be a dangerous distraction. There's a lot of things phones can make people end up doing that aren't . . . wise.

For example, people do ridiculous things for the most cool and impressive selfie possible. Why's that bad? Well, use your phone to look up the Wikipedia article 'List of selfie-related injuries and deaths' and read

14. By accident. I wasn't *aiming* for them.

about young people who were hit by trains or fell off cliffs. All for the sake of a cool profile pic.

Then there are trends, on TikTok or YouTube or whatever, that are actively dangerous. Like that 2018 one which involved eating washing machine pods, despite them being *really* toxic. That's why you should NEVER, EVER DO THAT!

Biology doesn't care how many likes you get on a video;
if you eat poison, you'll be poisoned. And that's definitely 'unhealthy'.

And let's not forget that *other people* can end up injuring you, thanks to your phone.[15] Those physically present in the world around you are still, you know, *there*. Some seem to get so consumed by what's happening on their phone they forget this.

That's why you get people doing stupid and insensitive things with their phones. Like taking wacky selfies next to the deceased at funerals or at solemn memorial sites.

15. I don't mean me and my car. I've never actually hit anyone, I promise!

Or setting up annoying photo shoots in the middle of busy streets, at popular tourist locations or on a train station platform.

The point is, someone might think what they're doing via their phone is more important than the feelings and needs of those around them. But other people might not agree. I'm not saying that anyone would be right to punch the inconsiderate phone user in the face. But, thanks to a phone, it's certainly a *possibility*. And not one that's good for anyone's health in the long run.

'SO . . . ARE MY PARENTS RIGHT? ARE PHONES BAD FOR YOUR HEALTH?'

In a sense, your parents are right. There are several ways that our phones do make us unhealthier. But then, serious injuries are far more likely when you do stuff like play football or ride bikes, compared to messing about with your phone. Yet parents mostly *encourage* you to play football or ride a bike and get annoyed when you play on your phone.

This seems even more weird when you consider that

any harm to your body caused by phones is normally not *that* serious. Although it shouldn't be ignored either because you're still young and growing, and the changes your body goes through can be more significant in the long run.

But a lot of the examples I've included here are behaviours encouraged or enabled by phones. These can also lead to some very unhealthy outcomes. Or some very healthy ones.

Ultimately, phones *can* be bad for your physical health. But they don't *have* to be. It depends on what you do with it. As long as you *and* your parents approach it thoughtfully, and with common sense, it should all turn out fine. Fingers crossed.

Of course, as we've seen, **getting parents to use common sense** can be a whole other matter . . .

'YOUR PHONE IS DRAINING YOUR BRAIN!'

Whether it's in person, in school assemblies, on TV, in newspaper articles or wherever, parents and adults are regularly moaning about the harm phones do to young people like yourself. But when they do, it's usually focused not on the harm they do to your body overall, but to *one particular part* of your body. Your brain.

Phones 'change' your brain. Phones 'drain' your brain. Phones reduce your brain's ability to do important, vital things. It seems many parents are convinced that these are *facts*.

But are they worrying *too much*? According to the science . . . yes. Mostly.

'HOW CAN A PHONE "DRAIN" YOUR BRAIN?'

I'd say the main reason adults say phones 'drain your brain' is . . . because it rhymes. It makes it a catchy and memorable phrase, one that looks good in newspaper headlines.

But is it *right*? Can a phone actually reduce what your brain can do?

In one way, yes.
By disrupting your sleep.

Sleep is vital for a healthy brain. A sleeping brain actually has a lot of work to do. Two tasks in particular are very important.

One is to get rid of all the waste that builds up over a day of brain activity.[16] An awake brain is made up of *billions* of neurons (aka brain cells), doing *billions* of complicated biological things, like sending signals between cells, creating new connections, constructing and deconstructing bafflingly complex networks and

16. This is explained in more detail in my first book, *Why Your Parents Are Driving You Up The Wall and What To Do About It*, which has a whole chapter on sleep and how important it is for you.

much more. And all these things produce waste products – like how fire produces ash and smoke. This junk builds up and can cause problems for brain cells, if not removed.

When we're asleep, our brain 'takes the bins out', clearing away this waste, allowing our brain cells to work better.

The second important task is processing and filing away all the new information and experiences our brains absorb during the waking day. A bit like in a library – putting new books onto the right shelves. Our brain does this while we sleep.

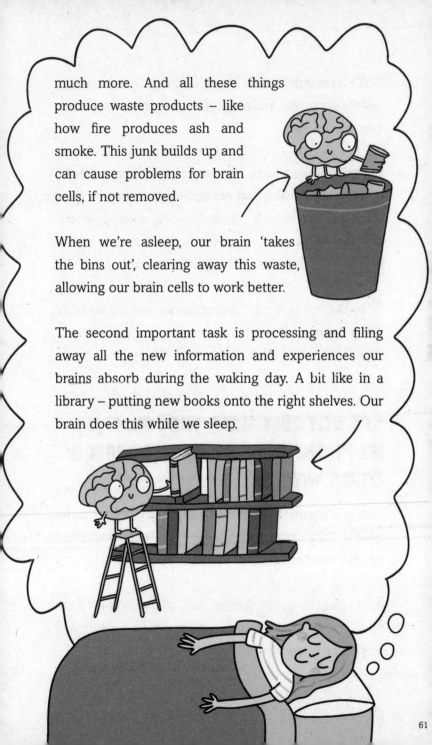

While researching this book, I spoke to many young people about this and most of them agreed that phones *keep you up late*.

Basically, your phone can 'drain' your brain just by keeping you awake. Not enough sleep makes us more forgetful, less able to concentrate, clumsier, grumpier and so on. If we don't sleep enough, our brains become less organized and more clogged with waste.

In fact, you could say that phones *prevent* your brain being drained (of waste). And that's even less helpful!

'IT'S NOT JUST SLEEP, THOUGH, IS IT? MY PHONE CAN "DRAIN" MY BRAIN IN OTHER WAYS.'

This is a common complaint, particularly among older adults. They worry your phone is 'draining' your brain by removing its ability to do important things.

According to your parents and grandparents, back in their day they could use their brains to do many incredible things like:

- **Recite long essays or poems from memory**

  TO BE OR NOT TO BE. **THAT** IS THE QUESTION.

- **Do quick calculations**

  IF IT'S 10 MILES TO MY HOUSE, AND MY BIKE GOES 30MPH, WHEN SHOULD I BE HOME?

- **Memorize facts, places and people**

  MY UNCLE LIVES IN PARIS, THE CAPITAL OF FRANCE. IT'S WHERE THE EIFFEL TOWER IS.

- **Solve problems using only their minds**

  I PROMISED TO MOW THE LAWN AT THE SAME TIME I SAID I'D MEET MY FRIENDS. SO WHAT I CAN DO IS . . .

- **Form lasting friendships and relationships, without any screens being involved**

  I CAN'T WAIT TO TELL MY BEST FRIEND ALL ABOUT WHAT JUST HAPPENED. I KNOW THEY'LL LOVE IT.

But young people today? You can't do any of that! (Again, according to those adults.) You don't need to remember anything, calculate anything, recall anyone's birthday or talk to anyone. Because your phone does it all.

As a result, many parents and older people believe that your brain won't develop properly because you rely on your phone to handle all the important stuff it would normally do. It's like a muscle that's never exercised, leaving you weak and feeble. Then you'll be *even more* dependent on your phone.

These worries aren't valid, though.

A lot of these fears come from older people getting mixed up between 'important stuff the brain does' and 'stuff *we* learned in school'. Maybe most young people today can't recite a whole thousand-word poem from start to finish from memory alone. But . . . why's that bad? Some adults make it seem like reciting poems is a really important thing for us to do – like being able to run. As if our ancient ancestors were fending off sabre-tooth tigers with ten-minute Shakespeare monologues.

The thing is, all these important things your brain does took *millions of years* to evolve. And they won't immediately disappear just because you look at Snapchat instead of sonnets. That's like saying, 'If kids keep riding bikes, eventually they won't be able to walk!' It's as daft as it sounds.

Sure, adults and parents can point to scientific studies showing that using your phone reduces your ability to memorize stuff, makes you more antisocial and isolated, makes it less easy to control emotions, affects your reading skills and more.

However, for every study which says phones 'drain' your brain, there's one saying the exact opposite – that they *enhance* your brain. Using your phone means dealing with lots of information, multiple conversations, several feeds at the same time. Your brain deals with all this, moment by moment, and studies show this can lead to

increased brain speed and connectivity, better multitasking, better memory, higher intelligence and so on.

Also, your brain needs resources to do everything it does. Like the energy stores in its cells and the complex chemicals and proteins that allow it to make new connections. Stuff like that. And it only has a limited amount of these resources at any one time.

Basically, your brain is not drained by phones. They don't suck these resources out of your head, like a straw in a milkshake. Rather the resources it has are diverted and used elsewhere. Like how if you ride a bike instead of walking, you're still using your legs. A lot. They don't just shrivel up because they're being used for something else – something a bit more high-tech than running.

The fact that there are lots of scientific studies that say completely different things when it comes to brains and phones shows just how complicated studying the brain is. The full effects of phones on your brain are still 'to be confirmed'. But what we can say is, your brain, and its ability to do stuff, is sturdier and more enduring than many concerned parents realize.

And the brain's abilities don't somehow 'go away' just because you learn different things to older people.

'OK, BUT IS MY PHONE CHANGING MY BRAIN?'

This is another thing many parents and adults worry about – and you may have heard it on the news or from their discussions with friends. That using your phone *changes* your brain.

And this is bad, right? After all, if phones made your lungs smaller or turned your skin green, that would be terrible. But they're actually changing your most important organ: your brain. So surely that's even worse? Nature made you a certain way, and any gadget that changes that is clearly something to be worried about.

Actually, if your brain didn't change at all after using a phone that would be far more worrying.

Because your brain changes *all the time.*

Everything your brain does depends on the connections between brain cells, called neurons. Every time we learn or experience something new, your brain responds to this by creating new connections or changing old ones. This is basically how it stores and uses information.

NEURONS

So the more you experience something, the more the physical structure of your brain actually changes.

Sure, prolonged phone use probably would lead to obvious changes in your brain. But the same applies to fishing. Or table tennis. Or playing instruments. You never hear parents whining about those things.

But even so, 'concerned' adults and parents keep insisting that any change to your brain that can be blamed on phones is bad. Why? Well, I'm sure they have their reasons (and we'll look at these in the next chapter). These reasons may not be based in actual science and evidence, but hey, that's parents for you.

'IF THAT'S ALL TRUE, I DON'T SEE WHAT THE PROBLEM IS.'

Funny you should say that, because if you're struggling to see things, that could well be a result of using your phone too much.

Remember earlier, when I talked about how my parents were certain that too much screen time would give me 'square eyes'? Well, if that did somehow happen, we'd go blind: the round shape of your eyes is vital for your ability to see. And the shape of your eyes is actually something that *can* be affected by using your phone too much.

Your eyes are actually part of your brain, like how your fingers are part of your arm. They're directly connected and are made of much of the same tissue (groups of cells). Take your retina, which is essentially a sheet of *brain cells* attached to the back of the eye (on the inside). When light enters our eyes through our pupils, it's projected onto the retina, like a tiny, squishy cinema screen. The retina cells are triggered by this light and send information to the brain. This gives us vision.

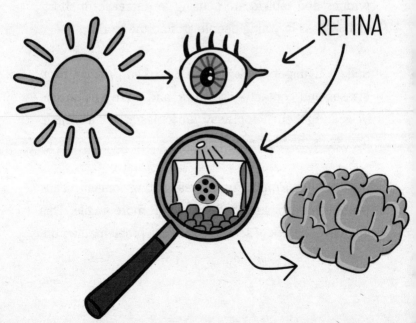

RETINA

Because of the physics of light, your eye's shape is really important for this process. But, like other body parts, the shape of your eyes can change, depending on what you make them do. Basically, your eye is *meant* to be round, like a football. But if you spend too long focusing on things up close, your eye can become longer (like a rugby ball, except not *that* long) because a longer eyeball is better for focusing on nearer things. Why? Again, physics.

And this becomes an issue when every young person has a device that they look at for hours every day, held a few inches from their face. In fact, many optometrists (highly trained eye scientists) are concerned that phones and tablets are causing an increase in short-sightedness in young people around the world.

Still, you might think this isn't so bad. We do have glasses and contact lenses now, and there's no shame in wearing them. People say you look smart, if anything. So what's the big deal?

It's not that simple. Your eyes getting longer means your retina gets stretched, making it more fragile. This increases the risk of serious eye health problems later on.

Overall, 'making it harder to see' is a change to the brain caused by phones. And not a helpful one.

'SO ARE PHONES GOOD OR BAD FOR MY BRAIN?'

That's a tricky question, because phones are bad for your brain *and* good.

The problem is, our brains do so much important stuff and phones interact with our brains in so many different ways. As a result, asking 'What do phones do to my brain?' is like asking, 'What does weather do to my town?' The answer is a *lot*, but a lot of different stuff. And some weather does the opposite of other weather (e.g. a heatwave dries out everyone's lawn, a thunderstorm fixes that).

To truly appreciate the whole 'phone vs. brain' thing, you'd need to look at specifics. And we'll be looking at how phones affect *something specific* about your brain, and what it does, throughout this book.

But for now, remember this: your parents are right to believe your phone can have unhelpful effects on your brain. But by focusing on *only* these unhelpful things, they're ignoring the many *good* things phones can do for your brain.

They'll also be ignoring just how tough and flexible your brain really is.

Also, by focusing just on the negatives, your parents are causing more stress for themselves, which leads to more arguments between them and you, which leads to more stress and so on . . .

The whole point of this book is to explain how phones affect you more clearly and prevent these arguments. But your parents may not be able to let go of all these gloomy ideas they have, so it's up to you to convince them.

Good luck with that!

'PHONES ARE BAD FOR YOUR (MENTAL) HEALTH!'

Despite everything we've covered so far, the worries your parents have about your phone doing you harm are mostly about your *mental* health. And they're right to be concerned (for once).

But the ways in which phones affect your mental health are much more complicated than most people realize. And by 'people', I mean your parents. It's so complex, we'll be coming back to it again and again in this book. But for now, let's cover some important basics.

'WHAT EXACTLY IS MENTAL HEALTH?'

Good question. Mental health is a very complex matter, with loads of different theories (and arguments) about it. But here's how *I'd* explain it.[17]

Your physical health is basically about how well your body is working and functioning.

By comparison, your mental health is about **how well your *mind* is working and functioning.**

Makes sense, right?

But also, your body has many different parts – blood, bones, nerves, guts, all that stuff – which *all* need to be working well for you to be in 'good' health. That's why, if you've a lung infection, kidney disorder or upset stomach, for example, you are 'unwell'. Even though it's just one body part going wrong. Everything is interconnected. It's like when a load of little kids play

---

17. A reminder that I'm a doctor of brains and have spent many years teaching all sorts of people all about mental health, so I like to think my take is a decent one.

together and one falls over and starts crying. Soon, they're all crying.

Similarly, there are various parts that make up your mind (thoughts, emotions, memories, instincts, logic, reason, to name a few), and if they're working OK, you've got decent mental health.[18] But again, if one part starts misbehaving, it affects everything else.

Your brain starts producing too much sadness? You end up with depression. Too much fear? You get anxiety. If your ability to think is compromised, you can lose track of what's real and what's not, which is what happens in delusions and stuff like that.

It's all connected too. Being constantly afraid, thanks to anxiety . . . that can really bring your mood right down, to the point where you can develop depression too.

So yeah, there are many similarities between mental and physical health. But also, many important differences. **However, they're both equally important.**

---

18. Some people call it 'well-being', but others use the phrases 'mental health' *and* 'well-being' to mean different things. To keep things simple, I'm going to assume they're the same thing, until I'm told otherwise.

It's also worth mentioning that all the things that make up mental health are things your brain does, so there's a lot of overlap between brain stuff and mental health stuff, as we'll see soon enough.

'OK, SO HOW DO PHONES AFFECT MENTAL HEALTH?'

Let's make this clear: your phone can indeed affect your mental health. Quite significantly. Does that mean your parents and all those other finger-wagging adults are right? Not exactly.

For one, it's unfair to single out phones. If you can experience it mentally, then it can affect your mental health. And we can experience *everything* mentally. Even things that haven't happened or don't exist. Have you ever been extremely anxious about something that hasn't happened? Like failing a test or asking your crush out on a date? Exactly.

This makes it hard to work out the exact cause of mental health problems. With physical illnesses, it's usually easier. Have they been picking fights with cage fighters? Eating raw chicken found in bins? Decided to lick their hands clean instead of washing with soap? If so, you can pinpoint how their health got worse.

But with a mental health problem, you must consider *everything they've experienced*.[19] And that's a lot. So, when talking about mental health in younger people, pointing at phones and bellowing

THERE'S THE PROBLEM.

will never be 100 per cent correct.

However, that doesn't mean you should ignore the impact your phone has. Having a phone means you can experience a whole range of things you never would have without it. And many of these can be less than helpful for your mental health. It's as if your phone opens an interdimensional gateway which allows a load of unfamiliar critters to scamper through and start gnawing on your mental health.

OK, maybe that's a bit of a weird metaphor. But consider this:

19. In psychiatry, it's called 'the biopsychosocial model'.

Would there be so many young people with body image issues if it weren't for Instagram constantly bombarding you with filtered pictures of beautiful people?

Would online bullying be such a problem if young people weren't constantly online?

Would young people stay up until 1am on a school night talking to their friends if they had to do it in person?

The likely answer, to all these questions, is no.

We'll be looking further into all this, and more, later in this book. But for now, it's hard to deny that phones can indeed have a big impact on your mental health.

'HASN'T IT BEEN PROVEN BY SCIENCE THAT PHONES ARE BAD FOR OUR MENTAL HEALTH?'

You might have heard many adults say that phones are damaging young people's mental health as if it's a cast-iron fact. And many will point to research and data revealing that the number of mental health problems in

young people has increased a lot
since smartphones were introduced.

And that proves it, right? Phones harm
young people's mental health.

Earlier I pointed out that mobile phones being
introduced *didn't* lead to an increase in brain tumours,
so the idea that they cause brain tumours must be
wrong. By the same logic, if mental health issues
increased soon after phones became common, then
that means they *are* bad for mental health, right?

You could certainly use this argument, and many people
do. It's not so simple, though. All this proves is that the
number of recorded mental health problems in young
people is increasing, and have been since the mid-
2000s, around the time smartphones were introduced.

However, have you heard of 'correlation is not
causation'? It's a short-but-geeky way of saying that

just because two things happen
at the same time, this does
not automatically mean that
one is responsible for the other.

For example, in the summer months, sales of ice cream and sunblock go up at the same time. Does this mean ice cream is burning people's skin? No. People buy ice cream and sunblock *because it's sunny*! That's the cause. Hot weather. The fact that two things look like they're connected does not automatically make it so.

It's the same for phones and mental health problems. There may be a connection, but there are *many* possible factors that could explain the rise in numbers beyond 'phones make you mentally unwell'.

One factor could be that medicine is constantly getting better at spotting and diagnosing mental health problems in young people, so you'd expect to see more of them recorded. Like how you can see more things in the dark when you put night-vision goggles on.

Or another could be that the internet has given young people far more access to information about mental health, so people can more easily recognize when they've got issues that they should seek help with and then get a diagnosis.

Or, since the mid-2000s, young people have been exposed to crisis after crisis – from the environment to the economy to politics. None of these are down to young people, but they'll have to deal with them eventually. With all the stress and worry that will lead to, it would be amazing if the mental health of young people *didn't* suffer.

If we're being cynical, that could explain why adults (the ones mostly responsible for all these problems) are so keen to blame phones. They're an easy target . . . despite all the other things that could cause mental health problems in young people and all the evidence showing that phones are often good for their mental health.

'HANG ON . . . PHONES CAN BE GOOD FOR OUR MENTAL HEALTH?'

Pretty much. I said phones affect your mental health; I never said it was only in a *negative* way.

While there are plenty of studies saying phones harm your mental health, there are just as many saying they improve it. In various ways.

Yes, phones expose you to cyberbullying and trolling . . . but also give you a way to easily express yourself and receive positive feedback and affirmation.

Yes, your phone allows you to see countless people who make you feel rubbish . . . but also connects you with others who might be feeling the same way and can help you find communities of friends and people who share the same interests as you.

Your phone may stop you having as much face-to-face contact with people . . . but it also means you can speak to friendly individuals all over the world.[20]

20. Phones are so common now that *not* having one can mean you're overlooked or excluded (even if unintentionally) by your friend group. And that's also not so good for your mental health.

Phones are particularly good for connecting you with people and resources to help with tricky personal issues, like sexuality, gender, drugs and, yes, mental health. It's often hard to talk to your parents about these things. Not because of anything they've done, just because the relationship you have with your parents means it's easier to speak to a sympathetic stranger about deeply personal things. At least at first.[21] And if you can do that in a safe, controlled way, via your phone? Even better.

In general, if you take all the studies into how phones affect your mental health and combine them, it looks like phones have no significant effect on the mental health of young people. But it's not that phones *can't* affect mental health. Rather, it's because they have as many helpful impacts as they do harmful ones, so they basically cancel each other out.

21. Again, the whole parent–child relationship, when it comes to this stuff, is explored in my previous book, *Why Your Parents Are Driving You Up The Wall And What To Do About It.*

'SO *WHY* IS IT DIFFICULT TO TALK ABOUT MENTAL HEALTH WITH MY PARENTS?'

Lots of reasons. Many of which we'll explore soon. But here's one that not many people understand.

Despite mental health existing as long as humans themselves, it's only been a few decades since it was properly recognized as 'a thing'. We know now that stress and trauma can affect your mind so much that you can't even function, but until relatively recently this idea never even *occurred* to most people, leading to much . . . unpleasantness.[22]

Thankfully, people have been working hard to fix this. Which means you've probably heard a lot about mental health already, particularly in school.[23] This likely didn't happen for your parents.

This means that we've ended up in a weird situation. It's your parents' job to look after and care for your mental health (because they're, you know . . . *your parents*), but you often *know more about mental health than them.*

---

22. I don't want to spoil the vibe, so just trust me when I say the history of mental health treatment, or lack thereof, is . . . bleak.
23. If everything in this section is stuff you've heard before, sorry. But it's best to be sure.

And this can be frustrating! For you, particularly.

It's like your parents are giving you driving lessons, **but you're the one with a licence.**

And it can mean your parents end up saying and doing things, supposedly for the sake of your mental health, that you don't agree with. Sometimes your parents can be overly concerned about mental health matters. Other times, not enough.

As we've seen, they are clearly worrying too much when they focus entirely on the harmful effects phones have on your mental health and completely ignore the good things. Which is like banning you from learning to ride a bike because you could fall off and get injured. While that's true, it ignores all the benefits of bikes. All the exercise, fresh air, fun . . .

You lose out on so much if you only ever focus on possible downsides.

On the other hand, parents can be far too chilled about mental health stuff. For example, have they ever told you you're *addicted* to your phone because you use it so much? A lot of adults happily throw this term around.

But addiction is a medical term for serious mental health conditions. It is usually used when we refer to substances like drugs and alcohol. *Not* excessive use of phones.

This isn't to say that your phone use *isn't* a problem. It could well be. But it's highly unlikely to be an actual *addiction*.[24] And calling it one both makes you using your phone sound much worse than it is, and makes serious mental health problems sound far less serious.

If parents referred to every bump, bruise and scrape as 'a broken leg', that would be scary and confusing, while also meaning people with broken legs got less concern and sympathy. This is the same thing, but for mental health.

24. There are barely a handful of cases of what could be called smartphone addiction. And even they are debatable.

These are just some of the examples of how, even if they have the best possible intentions, your parents' understanding of mental health can be a bit limited. And they can end up blaming things that they arguably shouldn't. Like your phone.

'THAT'S . . . A LOT TO THINK ABOUT.'

Tell me about it. I spent nearly a decade teaching many parents, even *grandparents*, about mental health, as an adult qualified to do exactly that. And it wasn't easy. So it's going to be even more of an uphill struggle for you and other young people to deal with your parents well-meant-but-often-unhelpful efforts to protect your mental health.

There are just *so many ways* your phone can affect your mental health. Because there is so much you can do with it. And from your parents' perspective, the whole discussion around mental health is very new to them. And when you're an adult, new things can scare you and make you behave weirdly.

CHAPTER 2

'BACK IN MY DAY, WE DIDN'T HAVE PHONES!'

'THESE NEW-FANGLED GADGETS . . .'

So we've explored some of the more obvious worries your parents have about your phone and what effect it has on you. And we've seen how many of these worries don't hold up to closer inspection.

But let me be clear here: I'm *not* saying that your parents are idiots or fools.[25] The truth is, there are good reasons why your parents are (mostly) in charge and not you.

Again, I'm not saying *you're* an idiot or a fool either. You're clearly not.[26] But you *are* much younger than your parents. And like it or not, this makes a big difference. It means your parents have much more experience and understanding of the world and how it works. Because

25. I mean . . . they *could* be. But *I'm* not saying that. I don't even know them!
26. You're currently reading a book written by a brain doctor! How non-idiotic can you get?

of this, they're the ones making decisions on your behalf – as they've had more time to figure stuff out.

Except, that's not always true, is it? There are times when your parents' age and experience make their understanding *worse*. And that's particularly true when it comes to phones and new technology.

'SO MY PARENTS CAN'T UNDERSTAND PHONES AND MODERN TECH?'

It's not that parents don't *understand* phones. They do. They've probably got their own, which they use fine. It's more that they can't help but see phones as something automatically *bad*. Especially when it comes to the effects they have on their child.

And that's you.

In fairness, your parents aren't being *totally* unreasonable. As we saw just now in the previous chapter, there *are* things for your parents to worry about when it comes to young people using phones. But these *possible* negative effects phones can have –

they're just one side of the story. And many parents aren't very interested in hearing about the other side, the one that shows that your phone can be both useful and beneficial.

Imagine if your parents only ever watched the first half of superhero movies. So they see all the stuff about evil aliens destroying cities or criminal masterminds putting their evil plans in motion, but nothing about the heroes, in colourful skin-tight suits, swooping in to save the day. It makes for a *very* different viewing experience.

If they then kept telling you off for watching superhero movies because 'They're just confusing and depressing,' that would be silly, right? But that's basically what countless parents do with phones: focus on the negatives, ignore the rest.

And this negative view of phones, this fear and suspicion, is usually the result of age and experience.

'BEING OLDER MAKES YOU *SCARED* OF TECHNOLOGY? ARE YOU SURE THAT'S RIGHT?'

Yeah, pretty sure. For parents (and adults generally), being paranoid about 'new' technology is something that's been happening for a long time. And it's not just about phones.

Consider the following quote:

> . . . *it will implant forgetfulness in their souls; they will cease to exercise memory because they rely on that which is written, calling things to remembrance no longer from within themselves, but by means of external marks.*

In the last chapter, we saw that many parents worry your phone could be making a right mess of your memory: with a phone, you don't *need* to rely on your brain to remember things. This quote says the same thing: people won't need memory any more, as they can 'rely on that which is written' (on their phone screen, for example), without needing to access information 'from within' (as in, within their brain).

Granted, the language in this quote is . . . more 'flowery' than we might be used to. But that's because it wasn't said by an angry newspaper writer. It was said by Socrates, an ancient Greek philosopher who lived *two and a half thousand years ago*!

What sort of 'new' technology from *that* deep in history got Socrates so worked up? Sundials? Underpants? The latest model iStone?

No, it was *writing*. Yes, writing. Putting words on paper, to read them again later. It was a new thing back then and Socrates genuinely feared it would cause people's memories to shrivel and die from lack of use.[27]

WRITING WILL BE THE RUIN OF CHILDREN, MARK MY WORDS!

27. There's a different Socrates quote in my previous book, where he whines about young people being lazy and having no respect for their elders. He seemed to have real issues with young people and change. Unfortunately, Socrates was eventually executed. His crime? 'Corrupting the youth'. True story. (The Ancient Greeks weren't *that* enlightened.)

Can you imagine saying to your teachers:

I CAN'T DO MY HOMEWORK BECAUSE WRITING DESTROYS YOUR MEMORY.

They'd say you were ridiculous. And if they did, they're technically saying they're smarter than Socrates, a world-renowned philosopher who basically *invented thinking*!

'BUT PEOPLE BELIEVED A LOT OF WEIRD STUFF BACK THEN.'

Indeed. And this isn't the *only* example of smart people being unreasonably paranoid about new technology.

Renowned scientist Conrad Gessner said, in one of his books, that the modern world gave people too much access to information, which is 'confusing and harmful' to the mind. The sort of things adults say about phones and the internet all the time.

Conrad Gessner, though, lived five centuries ago. Not as long ago as old 'writing is the devil!' Socrates, but still.

And rather than smartphones, he was warning everyone about the dangers of the printing press, the invention that allowed books, pamphlets, etc. to be made quickly and in big numbers and sent round to everyone and anyone. In fact, many 'leading thinkers' at the time feared the poor lower classes would fry their brains if they could just read books whenever they wanted.

Because, as we all know, there's nothing worse for your brain than reading books, right?

It gets better. In 1883, an official medical journal article warned everyone about the damage that would be inflicted on young people by another invention, which would 'exhaust the children's brains and nervous systems', as well as 'ruin their bodies by protracted imprisonment'. As in, being forcefully kept in one place, for a long time.

What was this new thing?

Schools.

'WAIT . . . SCHOOLS? ACTUAL SCHOOLS?'

Yes, actual schools. When public schools were introduced, many doctors and scientists were *convinced* they were bad for children's mental and physical health.[28] Indeed, the medical experts of the day believed 'excessive study' was a cause of madness. The fact that you need 'excessive study' to become a medical expert was never mentioned.

My point is, many modern parents worry that phones are bad for you because they get in the way of important, healthy things, like reading, writing, studying and school.

But at some point in history, each of those things was a modern invention. And parents, adults and experts all insisted they were harmful to children. The complete opposite of what parents believe today.

Are you seeing a pattern here?

---

28. Although schools could be way harsher and more brutal in the past, so they might have had a point.

'BUT . . . SCHOOLS AND READING AND WRITING, THEY'RE NOT *PROPER* TECHNOLOGY.'

Fair point. Most people would consider 'technology' to mean machines, devices, gadgets, things involving metal, moving parts, electricity, stuff like that. But those things got people really worked up too. More so, if anything, because they tended to be even more complicated – and mysterious.

When steam trains were introduced, people became convinced that travelling over 30 miles per hour would crush the human body.[29]

The very first phones, the 'metal box attached to the wall' types, resulted in newspaper articles shouting about how they'd ruin our privacy and leave us all like lumps of jelly.

When records and rock and roll first became popular, countless parents honestly believed it was the work of the devil.

---

29. To illustrate how wrong this is, the astronauts on Apollo 10, one of the original moon missions, travelled *826 times faster than 30mph* and were fine.

And then there's the whole 'mobile phones give you tumours' thing, which I think I mentioned already.

It's even happened to me. When I was in school, there was a period when newspapers kept insisting that games consoles were making us kids violent. And these were old-school video games, which meant adults and parents thought colourful-blocky games about mushroom-squashing plumbers or hyperactive blue hedgehogs were reaching into our brains and turning us into murderers.

It wasn't true, of course. It hardly ever is.[30] But it keeps happening.

It seems like *any* new technology quickly leads to adults and parents angrily shaking their fists at it for being dangerous.

30. However, not *all* paranoia about new things is automatically wrong. Like the invention of the lobotomy got a *Nobel prize*! Meaning some dubious doctor said, 'If you stab people in the brain, they stop moaning,' and the scientific elite said, 'Genius, have a medal!' People weren't paranoid *enough* in this case.

'THIS IS STILL HAPPENING NOW?'

Absolutely. Like I said, many fears and anxieties your parents have around phones will come from this suspicion adults seem to have about new technology.

And there's always something new popping up for them to freak out over. As I write this, you can't go ten minutes without a news article or programme or podcast or announcement about the dangers of artificial intelligence (AI). It's going to do so many awful things, like read your secret, innermost thoughts, kill off all culture, take away everyone's jobs, even destroy civilization.

Of course, if you speak to more level-headed experts, they'll urge everyone to calm down and get a sense of proportion. What people are currently calling AI has actually been around for years. It's been running your online advertising algorithms, for instance.

What on earth do I mean by that? Well, you know how you might buy, say, a pen online? And then constantly get ads for pens in your feeds? It's a type of 'AI' doing that. It's saying, 'They just bought a pen,

they're probably starting a massive pen collection, so I'd better show them countless options.'

In fairness, your parents are probably the ones usually buying stuff online, so they'll be the ones getting such ads. And it's another thing that might get them annoyed at phones.

Granted, advertising algorithms aren't the *only* form of AI you get. And they're more annoying than dangerous, at least.

Again, this doesn't mean AI is totally safe or won't ever cause serious problems.

It's a tool and it depends on how it's used. And **who** is using it.

Some seem to want to use it to put writers and artists out of work by generating new 'content' on command. Others seem to think it's totally fine to use AI to make political, economic, even military decisions that affect many lives.

Sure, there are also plenty of ways AI could be, and is, used positively.[31] But, predictably, most adults and parents head straight to the worst-case 'doomsday' scenario.

Which stresses them out. So they get even more worked up, and even more paranoid, and the cycle continues.

'OK, *WHY* DOES THIS HAPPEN?'

Ah, now we get to the good stuff.

Here's the thing: your brain has a lot to do if it wants to work in the modern world. It's got to make decisions, plan, react and respond to whatever's happening and more. It does all this and much more, *constantly*.

To make this even slightly possible, your brain needs a sort of baseline that includes information and understanding of how the world works. This is called the *mental model*, because your brain is running a constant mental simulation, a 'model', of how everything around

31. I remember reading about an advanced algorithm that was originally engineered to tell the difference between croissants, pretzels, biscuits, etc. in a busy bakery shop, but is now used to quickly recognize and diagnose cancer cells.

you 'works'. And it makes decisions according to what this model says.

It's a bit like the operating system on your phone. For example, if you've an iPhone, it's run on iOS. You can put many apps and photos and files on your phone, but it's the operating system that tells your phone how to work ('operate') these programmes and where they go.

Your mental model is basically your mind's operating system.
It lets you make sense of all the things you experience.

Now, your mental model isn't downloaded into your brain over the Wi-Fi; instead, it's assembled over many years. It's like a bubbling stew of your important memories, experiences, beliefs, attitudes and assumptions. Particularly those picked up during your teenage years.

And then, when you're a 'mature' adult, your brain looks at the mental model you've built up and thinks, 'Yeah, that'll do,' and that's what you use to navigate life from then on. So if you've had a job for a few years, you'll have a mental model of what to do, how to behave, at work. Your mental model tells you to turn up at 8:30 a.m. to wear smart clothes, where to sit, who to collaborate with, who to avoid – all that.

This is part of the reason why your parents get to be responsible for stuff and you don't. You're still figuring out your mental models for how things in the world work and how to deal with them. Which, obviously, means you can't be sure if you're making the right decisions.

But your parents are further along, so they have established, 'finished' mental models for how things should work.

And there's the problem.

'WAIT, WHY IS THAT A PROBLEM?'

Adults *can* update their mental model by learning and experiencing new things after they mature. But it takes a long time and it's often just tweaks and adjustments.

For many, their understanding of the world, their mental model, is rather 'fixed'.

But you know what *isn't* fixed?

The world.

It keeps changing, progressing, advancing. Often in ways that many adults can't get their head around. Phones are a good example of this.

For many parents, their mental model, which tells them:

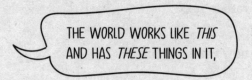

THE WORLD WORKS LIKE *THIS* AND HAS *THESE* THINGS IN IT,

was in place before smartphones came along. So to them, phones are 'not normal'. They're things to be wary and suspicious of, as is anything else that challenges their understanding of how the world works. Or *should* work.

This doesn't apply to young people like you. Your mental model is still under construction and smartphones have been part of your life since day one. Why would you be suspicious of them? It's like asking your parents if they're suspicious of trees.

'IS THAT WHY WE'RE ALWAYS DISAGREEING ABOUT MY PHONE?'

It's probably not the *only* reason, but it will certainly be something that plays a part. You and your parents, because of your age differences, see phones in completely different ways.

Here's another quote, from another historical genius. It's a more recent one, from legendary (to people my age) comedy writer Douglas Adams:[32]

> *Anything that is in the world when you're born is normal and ordinary and is just a natural part of the way the world works.*
>
> *Anything that's invented between when you're fifteen and thirty-five is new and exciting and revolutionary and you can probably get a career in it.*
>
> *Anything invented after you're thirty-five is against the natural order of things.*

To clarify, by 'against the natural order of things', he means wrong, weird, unnatural, just shouldn't happen. It sums up the situation with mental models and technology alarmingly well.

You might think that, because you're young and switched on, this won't happen to you. And it won't. Not for a while.

---

32. He wrote *The Hitchhiker's Guide to the Galaxy*. If you've not read it yet, I thoroughly recommend it. Only don't watch the movie version first.

But you may have your own children one day. And at some point in the future, they'll be as old as you are now. And who knows what kind of weird tech they'll be into then?

Perhaps they'll want the latest holographic interface chip implanted directly into their eyeballs. Or maybe the trendy way to watch YouTube shorts will be by licking Wi-Fi-compatible frogs. Will you, as a parent, be 'cool' with that?

Thing is, though – even if you say 'yes', and that you won't change your mind . . .

Sometimes the world changes faster **than your mind does.**

Just ask your parents.

'THINGS WERE BETTER WHEN I WAS YOUNGER!'

Many parents are suspicious and worried about your phone. That's just a fact.

Here's another thing those parents often think is a fact: their childhood was better than yours. *Their* childhood was full of carefree fun and healthy activities. Meanwhile, *your* childhood is you sitting indoors all day, staring at your screens and devices. And that's just awful. For you.

Many parents believe this is a fact. They bring it up regularly. They'll even post memes about it on Facebook. Which is a bit rich, isn't it? Criticizing your children for spending too much time online . . . by constantly going online to moan about it? But as we saw earlier, nobody said parents had to make sense.

But . . . are these parents *right*? Is your phone ruining your childhood? Actually, is your childhood being ruined *at all*? Was your parents' childhood really so much better than yours?

If you look at the actual evidence, the answer is . . . no. Look at the history of when your parents were young.

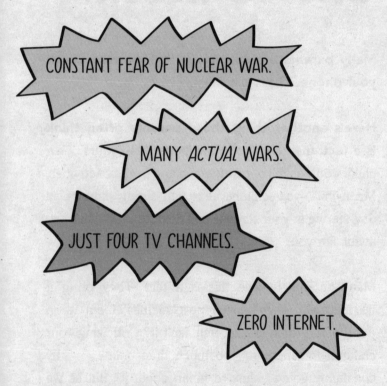

CONSTANT FEAR OF NUCLEAR WAR.

MANY *ACTUAL* WARS.

JUST FOUR TV CHANNELS.

ZERO INTERNET.

Being a kid with all that going on surely wouldn't be the biggest barrel of laughs.

But the strange truth is, *every* generation of parents seem to think their childhood was the best, no matter what. There were probably children in 1745 who were constantly being told by their parents how much better life was back 'in their day'.

It's yet another thing adults end up doing without realizing.

'OK, SO *WHY* DOES IT HAPPEN?'

When parents say that life was better 'in their day', they usually mean 'when they were younger'.

That's obviously a big part of it. They think things were better when they were younger . . . *because* they were younger. Of *course* you'd think life was better when you had much more free time and energy, and all your hair, and you could get out of a chair without having back spasms.[33]

It's more than that, though. Many adults insist their childhood was better, even when they also admit it was *awful*. For example, my grandparents would constantly

33. Why, yes, this *does* all apply to me.

go on about how, when they were kids, they had to walk for miles to school, every day. For miles. Through wind, rain, snow, wolves and . . . landmines? Probably. I don't know, I stopped listening eventually.

But then, within minutes, they'd turn round and say:

SCHOOL DAYS?
BEST DAYS OF YOUR LIFE!

How? *Why?*[34]

And there's the key question. *Why* do parents and adults insist their childhood was better than yours? Even if the evidence says otherwise.

Let's get one thing clear here: your parents very likely *do* believe their childhood was better. It's not that they're lying to you. No, it's more that *their brains are lying to them*.

---

34. I couldn't help but wonder: if the best days of their life included a hellish slog to be taught fractions by teachers who could hit you with sticks, how bad is their life *now*? From what I could see, my grandparents spent most of their days drinking tea and gardening. Which seemed . . . fine?

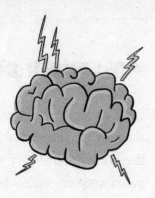

'YOUR BRAIN CAN *LIE* TO YOU?'

Oh, 100 per cent.

Your typical brain spends a lot of time lying to you about all manner of things. A lot of those things will be explored later in this very book. But while it's true that lying to other people is generally bad, when your own brain lies to you, it's often a *good* thing. It can be an important part of good mental well-being.

And as you get older, one of the things your brain ends up lying to you about **is your childhood**.

Or the past in general. It tells you that it was *better* than the present. Even when that's clearly not the case.

'HOW DOES IT DO THAT?'

OK, so your brain remembers things by storing them as memories. I think we can all agree on that?[35] However, the brain's memory doesn't work like the memory on your phone or a computer. Brains don't save information and just leave it as is, untouched, until it's needed later.

No. Your brain is constantly reorganizing and tweaking and updating and removing stuff from your memory. This means your memories *change* over time. And there are many automatic processes in your brain that make this happen.

One of these is called 'the fading affect bias', which describes how, in the typical human brain, bad or unhappy memories fade faster than good and happy ones.

Our strongest memories usually have a clear *emotional* quality. Which means that some of your strongest memories will be positive and make you feel happy when you remember them (e.g. your first Christmas,

---

35. In order to become a doctor, I spent five years researching how the brain forms memories, so you can probably trust me on this.

when you asked someone out and they said yes, when you got your first phone, etc.).

YIPPEEEEEE!
MY FIRST PHONE!

But, of course, other strong memories will be negative and make you feel sad/angry/ scared when you remember them (e.g. a pet dying, asking someone out and getting rejected, when you dropped your first phone down the drain, etc.).

But remember, *negative* emotions disappear from the memory faster than the positive emotions, which hang around much longer.

'BAD MEMORIES JUST DISAPPEAR?'

Not quite. The *memory itself* – the information about what happened – stays put. But the *emotions*, the *feelings* that memory triggers, they go away.[36]

36. Although research shows that your brain *does* regularly get rid of memories. But it's not *bad* memories that are removed; it's unused ones. Like, if you found a three-year-old blurry image of your own thumb in your phone's gallery, you'd just delete it, right? Your brain does the same with memories. Sometimes things just take up space.

Think of it like this: a memory is like chewing gum and the emotions it contains are the flavour. Some flavours are nice, like blueberry or candy floss, and some are awful, like battery acid or toilet water.

With the nice chewing gums, the flavour sticks around for ages. Maybe your whole life. With the unpleasant ones, the flavour vanishes quickly.

But in both cases, *you've still got the gum!* It's just that the gum that makes you go

still does that, but the gum that originally made you go

now makes you go

'SO MY PARENTS HAVE BRAINS FULL OF CHEWING GUM?'

Well . . . no. Obviously not.

What they *do* have is brains full of memories. *Old* memories. Because they're older people. And the older a memory is, the longer the bad emotional flavour has had to fade away, while the good emotional flavours hang around.

And the oldest memories your parents have will, logically, be *from their childhood*. Which means that all the bad stuff from then will have faded from their minds, but all the good stuff is still there. And so adults like your parents end up thinking their childhood was great. Even if they *didn't think that at the time*.

But your parents' more recent memories, from present day (which is *your* childhood) – those memories still have plenty of negative flavour left. So obviously, in your parents' minds, the past (their childhood) is clearly much better than the present (yours). This is a big part of why many parents insist their childhood was better. Even when it obviously wasn't.

'BUT *WHY* DOES THE BRAIN DO THIS?'

It may seem like a weird glitch, but this is something the brain's evolved to do over many millions of years.

'SO, PRESUMABLY, THERE'S A POINT TO IT?'

Yes, there is.

You may have heard people say, 'time heals all wounds'? Well, that's mostly true.[37] And this is part of that process. If you have a *physical* wound, your body repairs the damage, eventually. Otherwise it'll just keep causing non-stop pain and that's no good to anyone.

But not every wound is physical. They can be mental too, thanks to unpleasant and traumatic experiences. And these things are stored in your memory. And while nobody *enjoys* remembering grim experiences, it's still important. It means you can learn to avoid similar things happening again.

---

37. Obviously, there are some wounds, either physical or mental, which don't just 'get better' over time. They need help. This help might be medicine or therapy.

It's another thing our brains evolved to do, because it helped us survive. If some distant ancestor of ours spent four days vomiting after eating too many of a certain berry, that would obviously be something they'd rather forget. But if they encountered the same berries and didn't remember their multi-day puking party, they'd probably just eat them again. And this time it might get worse than throwing up.

And while it's a necessary process, you don't want it to go overboard. If bad memories didn't eventually fade, but kept on making you remember, and relive, unpleasant experiences, that would be the mental health equivalent of constantly being punched on your still-broken arm.[38]

So your brain makes sure that doesn't happen by making negative emotions fade from memory as quickly as it can.

---

38. This is actually what happens in post-traumatic stress disorder (PTSD) and is why it's so harmful. It's when the brain *can't* move on from or neutralize painful memories so keeps reliving them over and over.

'THAT ACTUALLY SOUNDS LIKE A GOOD THING.'

It certainly can be. At the very least, it prevents you from being too badly affected by unpleasant experiences, which strengthens your mental health.[39]

But it has downsides. It means as you get older, nostalgia (looking back at the past more fondly than you really should) happens more often, so has a much bigger impact on how you see the modern world, which affects your thinking and decisions.

Now, here's the thing to remember: if your parents are constantly saying their childhood was better than yours, that's probably because *they want you to have a good childhood*. That's the number-one priority for the typical parent!

But despite their best efforts, their brain is constantly telling them that your childhood is not as good as theirs. And that's not a nice thought for any parent who wants their kid to be happy.

---

39. Although depression, anxiety and things like that can interrupt this process. It's not a guarantee.

So what can they do about it? Can they change all the complex things that make your childhood different from theirs? No, they can't. It would be ridiculous to expect them to.

However, another thing your standard brain likes is easy answers and simple solutions. So rather than tackling all the world's present problems (which would be *really* hard), your average parent brain will often say, 'What's the difference between my childhood and my children's? Is there one obvious thing that's different about their childhood that's affecting them, that never affected me?'

And then they'll see the glowing rectangle in your hand and go:

AH **HA**!

'SO *THAT'S* WHY PARENTS BLAME PHONES FOR "RUINING" MY CHILDHOOD?'

It's one explanation, sure.

In your parents' defence, they're not deliberately trying to be jerks. They probably just don't like the fact that they can't give you the childhood they had (or *thought* they had) and want something to blame for that, to make them feel better.[40]

Although, let's not be *too* generous. Many parents often get carried away and they can be pretty annoying about it.

Like I said, many parents will share posts and memes about their childhood being far better, which always feature stuff like pictures of kids playing outside and laughing gleefully, as they swing from trees, splash in streams, tumble down hills . . .

---

40. All this is probably taking place in the unconscious parts of their brain, so they probably don't even realize they're doing it.

But next to this picture will be another, usually of sulky young people, hunched over, staring mindlessly at their phones in poorly lit rooms, their slack faces illuminated only by the ghostly glow of screens.

Below these will be a message, saying something like:

While it may make those parents feel better, there are a lot of ways in which this is wrong.

'BUT THEY'RE *NOT* WRONG, ARE THEY? YOU JUST SAID THAT PHONES HAVE MADE CHILDHOOD VERY DIFFERENT.'

That's the thing: it's totally reasonable to say smartphones and similar tech has made modern childhood very *different*. But is it definitely *worse?* Not really.

Sure, many things about the modern world *have* got worse over time (the environment is an obvious example), but it's nonsense to insist that everything's gone completely downhill since the golden age of your parents' childhood. I say that as someone who was there for much of it.

And you know what's particularly annoying? All those parents who post 'SHARE IF YOU PLAYED OUTSIDE WHEN YOU WERE A KID AND NOT ON YOUR PHONE ALL THE TIME!' memes – they make it seem like *they had a choice!* As if there *were* smartphones around when they were young, but they *chose* not to use them. Because they were *proper* kids, with morals and discipline and stuff. And if they could do it all again, they'd do it exactly the same!

I promise, this is nonsense. If there *were* smartphones around during your parents' childhood, they would have used them just as much as you do. Maybe even more so. Your parents probably don't remember how it felt to be constantly bored, to have nothing to do, to have to sit through hours of religious TV shows on Sunday afternoons since *there was nothing else on*!

And that's because all those negative feelings about those times have been **buffed away by the brain's quirky memory systems.**

If you could somehow confront parents with the cold, hard facts about what life is really like now, what it was like in the past and, most importantly, how they felt about it *at the time*, I'm confident your childhood would seem clearly better, in many ways.

I know that. *You* know that. And, deep down, I bet your *parents* know that.

But if you're a parent, it's a lot easier to blame phones for everything and carry on with your day.

'YOU'RE TOO YOUNG FOR A PHONE!'

How old should you be before you get a phone?

You and your parents have probably had this discussion, repeatedly, without ever agreeing on an answer. It's a very common argument.

The people responsible for issues like this – politicians, doctors, scientists – have researched it and confirmed, officially, how old you should be before getting your own phone, right?

They haven't, though. Because it's much harder to do this than people think.

Of course, this means that, whenever a parent or adult insists you're 'too young' for a phone, they haven't decided this using facts and knowledge but gut feelings and guesswork. Nobody actually knows *for certain* what age is 'right' for getting your first phone.

It's why parents and young people argue about it so much!

'BUT YOU CAN BE TOO YOUNG FOR A PHONE, SURELY?'

Oh, totally.

Imagine a baby with their own phone. They'd just try to eat it, so you'd end up with an expensive device covered in drool and gum dents. Which would be disgusting.

And even though they can walk and talk and hold things pretty well, toddlers and *very* young children aren't really *mentally* developed. Their brains and minds haven't figured out how things work just yet. Which means they often just don't understand, or 'get', phones. They particularly don't get how *fragile* they are. So they should be kept away from them.

For the phone's sake, as much as the very young child's.

'ARE YOU SAYING *CHILDREN* ARE BAD FOR *PHONES*, NOT THE OTHER WAY AROUND?'

That's *exactly* what I'm saying.

If you've got small children in your life, you'll know they are . . . chaotic. And boisterous. And, often, *filthy*. Even if they don't mean to be.

For example, we humans are always shedding and regrowing our skin, particularly the protective outer layer, without us even realizing. Have you heard that fact that most dust in your house is dead human skin? It's true.

It's *especially* true if small children live there. Their skin's growing at a frantic rate, so they're shedding even more. They're like snakes, only gross.[41]

In fact, when touchscreen devices were first used in primary schools, they got very mucky, very quickly.

---

41. Snakes aren't slimy; they're dry, clean creatures who shed their old skin, when necessary, in one go. They don't constantly fling bits of it everywhere, like some horrible organic firework.

Because the small students were constantly covering them with dead skin. And . . . other stuff. Like drool and snot. And that's bad for touchscreens. And phones use touchscreens.

Out of curiosity, I asked other parents if they had any other good examples of small children making a mess of phones and devices. And they did *not* disappoint . . .

'Our four-year-old decided to watch the iPad in the bath. Literally in the bath!'

'My nephew kicked a football into his mother's iPad while trying to film himself with it!'

'I know someone whose kid chewed on their phone so much while teething that their saliva corroded the phone on the inside.'[42]

---

42. See, I *told* you this would be disgusting!

So, yes, children shouldn't have phones when they're *very* young. They make a right mess of them. And who's paying the price for this technological carnage? Parents! So you can see why they'd be a bit wary of the whole 'giving your child their own phone' idea.

'WE QUICKLY GROW OUT OF THIS STAGE, THOUGH, DON'T WE?'

Yes.

The young, developing mind learns things *very* quickly.

Child development usually follows a series of achievements, or 'milestones' (as parents say). Very early on, these involve things like eating solid food, sitting up by yourself and learning to walk, talk and hold a pencil properly. It's fairly obvious stuff.

However, many of the milestones that come after are more mental than physical. Learning to read, use grammar, do mental arithmetic, understand that other people have their own minds and own experiences that are different to your own, for example.

'Understanding that certain objects and devices are expensive and fragile' would be included in this.

You might take these things for granted *now*, but they're actually complex abilities or milestones that took your brain some time to figure out. And if you haven't figured them out yet, having your own phone probably isn't the best idea.

'DOESN'T EVERYONE HIT THEIR MILESTONES EVENTUALLY?'

Mostly, yes. Particularly the earlier ones.

There are many good reasons why someone may be unable to walk (injury, disease, complications from birth), but you never meet someone who can't walk because they 'never learned how'.

Usually, we hit our milestones in a certain order. Unfortunately, it's very hard (well, pretty much impossible) to know *in advance* at what age a child will reach these milestones. Some children walk earlier than the average age, some much later. Neither is wrong or right. It's just humans being human.

If it helps, think of childhood development as like a cross-country run:

there's a certain distance that everyone needs to cover to get to the finish, **but everyone will be running at different speeds.**

Our development is influenced by both how we're made and the experiences we have, so there are countless different things that could affect how fast we reach our milestones and in what way.

Our DNA, too much or too little of a certain chemical, some brain cells in a particular bit of the brain, a helpful adult or unhelpful child relative. All this and so much more can affect how we develop and how quickly.

And if you're neurodivergent (are autistic or have ADHD or similar), your brain will work in even more different ways. So trying to work out how quickly you'll reach your milestones is more confusing again.

Unfortunately, even though it's well beyond their control, many parents feel it's their responsibility. This can cause parents a lot of stress, when it really doesn't need to.[43] And it means they can get preoccupied or take a dim view about anything that may be affecting you hitting your milestones.

But this obsession with milestones isn't always the best approach for parents. Remember, I said your development is like a cross-country *run*, not *race*. Getting to the finish line first might get some cheers from annoyingly competitive parents, but it ultimately doesn't matter *when* you get there.

However, this also makes it hard to have specific expectations about development. Like, if someone said, 'Everyone doing the run should be at the halfway point after 78 minutes exactly,' that would be ridiculous. And in a way, saying, 'Every child should be mature enough for a phone at *this specific age*' is the same thing.

---

43. Check out the *Bluey* episode 'Baby Race' for a perfect example of this.

'BUT . . . *LOADS* OF THINGS HAVE AGE RESTRICTIONS, SO PEOPLE *MUST* KNOW WHAT IS AND ISN'T SAFE FOR KIDS AT CERTAIN AGES.'

You'd think so. But if you look at age restrictions more closely, you can see how confusing, inconsistent and *random* they often are.

Take age restrictions for films. Something you're probably very familiar with. In the UK, a film that contains multiple battle deaths, arms being cut off and actual *decapitation*, can be given a PG certificate (any child can see it if their parents are with them). But if there's a head-butt in it? No. That's too much and it needs stronger age restrictions.[44]

It doesn't end there. UK age restrictions say you can't vote, drive a car or drink a beer before the age of 17 or 18. Because you're too young and irresponsible. But you're *expected* to choose a university degree – which costs thousands and affects the rest of your life – at 17. Or younger. So you're responsible enough for that . . . but not for a beer? Weird.

---

44. This actually happened with the 2002 UK release of *Star Wars: Episode II – Attack of the Clones*, part of the prequel trilogy. If you haven't seen it, it's . . . not the best.

And that's just in *this* country. In others, age restrictions and laws are often very different. Even though, at the basic biological level, children develop in the same way and at similar speeds wherever they are.

It can seem like age limits and restrictions are just adults guessing.

'AGE LIMITS ARE JUST ADULTS AND PARENTS . . . MAKING STUFF UP?'

While it's fun to imagine this is the case, the adult world isn't *that* chaotic. Not yet.

And sometimes 'the science' isn't the best guide. For example, according to actual science, a human can be considered a 'biological adult' as soon as they hit puberty. So from about age *11*!

You might be an 11-year-old reading this and thinking:

THAT SOUNDS COOL!

But . . . is it? Would you want to have a job, look after a house, be responsible for all the bills, be the main person taking care of other children *right now*?

Much of adult life involves work and responsibilities. No sensible person would expect a child, one who's not yet even a teenager, to handle all that.

'I COULD HANDLE SOME RESPONSIBILITY IF MY PARENTS JUST LET ME!'

I'm sure you could.

But have you ever heard the phrase 'be careful what you wish for'? That applies here.

Many restrictions today are based on a time when young children *could* do those things. And it . . . didn't end well. For many reasons, people were a lot less concerned about children's well-being in the old days. This often led to very strange things happening.

Have you heard of Sir Stirling Moss? Born in 1929, he became one of the UK's most famous (if not *the* most famous) racing drivers. This probably had something to do with the fact that his father gave him his first car when he was *nine years old!*

Can you imagine that happening today? It would make the news – and someone would probably go to jail.[45]

But history is full of stuff like this. In the old days, for the longest time, it was normal for schoolboys to be given beer with their lunch.[46]

Basically, with enough time and progress (and a lot of stuff going wrong that people didn't want to keep happening), things get to a point where enough parents say, 'You know what, this is *bad* for our children. So let's put a stop to it.'

Even if they don't always make 100 per cent sense, **a lot of age restrictions exist for good reasons.**

45. In fairness, it wasn't exactly *normal* in 1938 either. The minimum driving age of 17 was introduced in 1930. But the Moss family were apparently very posh and rich. And if you were rich and posh back then, that meant rules didn't apply to you so much. Granted, that can still be the case now, but it's not so obvious these days.
46. Girls didn't get beer in school. Usually because they didn't go to school at all. This was the *really* old days.

So now you can't drink, smoke, vote, drive . . . until you're deemed 'old enough'.

It just sometimes takes a while for parents to figure out *when* you're old enough. And a lot of the time, there's not enough information to help make these decisions. So age restrictions end up being more of a 'best guess' thing. Especially when it comes to new and unfamiliar things. Which, in many parents' eyes, is what phones are.

'DOES THIS MEAN STRICT AGE LIMITS WILL BE PLACED ON PHONES EVENTUALLY?'

We can't rule that out. If some scientific study proves, for definite, that using a phone at a very young age causes lasting harm, then strict limits on phones would probably be introduced. And *very* quickly.

However, is that likely to happen? I'd say no. Phone use is *already* very common among young people, like yourself. And they've been studied *a lot*. Yet, despite some interesting results, nobody has yet proven that they do you lasting damage.[47] Certainly nothing like the damage caused by underage smoking, drinking, driving, etc.

Phones just do too much useful stuff and have become a normal part of everyday life. It's hard to see how we'd introduce strict age controls at this point without causing chaos. It would be like the government suddenly saying:

> **Going too fast is dangerous full stop, so you can only ride in a car or other vehicle when you're 18.**

Can you *imagine* the disruption that would occur if that happened? Every child would have to walk to school, parents could never drive them anywhere, holidays would no longer be a thing, parents would have to give up jobs. Our whole society would come screeching to a halt. Much like the cars themselves, in this case.

---

47. Despite how many parents and grumpy adults want this to be true.

'SO . . . WHAT AGE SHOULD YOUNG PEOPLE BE GIVEN PHONES?'

I don't know! Didn't you read any of what I just wrote?

(I'm kidding. Although many parents will do just that: patiently listen as someone explains that there's no real answer to a complex question and then say, 'Yeah, but what is the answer?' Honestly, it's annoying.)

I know what you mean, though. Even if there's no real useful information on when the right age is to have a phone, *is* there an age where most parents just, sort of, generally agree it's OK for their child to have their own phone?

Sort of. Scientific studies show show that, in the UK, at age 11, over 90 per cent of children have a phone of their own.

Why 11? Well, many reasons. At the biological level, that's usually the age when all the important changes you go through during your teens, to become 'mature', first start happening. Maybe parents can recognize that? On some level, maybe even an unconscious one, perhaps your parents realize that you're beginning a whole new stage of your life.

But it's also important because (in the UK, at least), it's the age when you go from primary to secondary school.

Any reasonable parent will know that's a huge deal. It's a major step in your growth and development. Another well-known milestone. Hopefully, they recognize it as a sign you're more mature, can handle more stuff. For example, a phone.

In fact, your parents may feel you actually *need* a phone to keep up with everything and everyone, and stay in contact with them as you go through this next big step.

So yes, at 11, your parents may actually *want* you to have your own phone.

You might think,

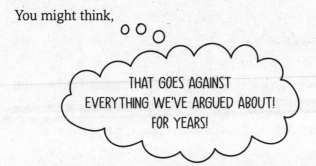

Yes, it does. But that's the thing about parents: nobody said they were consistent . . .

'YOU NEED TO PUT YOUR PHONE DOWN ... BUT I DON'T.'

Parents being wrong about phones so much would probably be less annoying if they were *consistently* wrong. If they stuck to the same lot of wrong rules and views and opinions, it'd be much easier to deal with.

But they don't.

Parents regularly change their minds, move the goalposts or tell you not to do something with your phone, then do it themselves. Right in front of you!

However, assuming your parents aren't deliberately being jerks, there *are* good reasons for it. Sometimes your parents being inconsistent can be *helpful*. Or it's meant to be, at least. It just doesn't *feel* like that.

So, to help better understand the strange adult brain, let's look at some common examples of where your parents say one thing about phones and do another. Or say one thing one day, then something else entirely the next, but still expect you to do as you're told.

For instance, why do your parents tell you off for using your phone too much, but use their own just as much, if not more, right in front of you?

'YEAH! WHAT'S THAT ABOUT?'

Actually, I need *you* to ask the question. Otherwise, this title format doesn't work.

'SERIOUSLY?'

Yeah. If you wouldn't mind.

143

'FINE . . . WHY DO MY PARENTS TELL ME OFF FOR USING MY PHONE TOO MUCH, WHEN THEY USE THEIRS EVEN MORE?'

Many parents say they're using their phone 'for work'. And maybe they are. Even if it's not for their actual job, they could be doing household tasks. Many everyday parenting jobs are done with a phone these days, like paying bills, contacting plumbers or ordering groceries.

But, just between us . . . there's no way that your parents are *always* using their phone for work.

Also, while the age it's safe to have a phone is up for debate (see previous section), nobody argues that *adults* are old enough. This might seem hugely unfair to you, but there is *some* logic to it.

The obvious argument is that your young brain is *still maturing*, still assembling your mental models of the world. Parent brains are not.

And like the teenage body, things done to a still-maturing brain, or the things it's made to do, can have a more lasting impact than with a mature brain. For example, if you use your phone to look up non-stop fun stuff for hours every day, you risk damaging your ability to focus and think about things in depth (or so some scientists believe). This is logically less likely to happen in an adult brain, which has already learned how to do those things.

In a way, using a phone, to a young person's brain, is like using a stick to draw rude words in wet cement; fun at first, but it'll soon set and leave something unpleasant forever.

But your *parents* using a phone, with their mature brains? Surely that's like trying to write a rude word in *dry* cement: you can push as hard as you like; it'll just break the stick. The cement will be fine.

It's an interesting idea. Only . . . it's not true.

Many scientific studies reveal that **an adult brain can be as affected by phones as a younger brain.**

Mental health issues and negative behaviours in adults can be made worse by using a phone a lot.

However, like we saw in the first chapter, it's not really the *time* spent on a phone that is the issue, but what it's used for. You can use your phone to read books, watch yoga videos, listen to chillout music for hours on end, and that's fine.

But use it to stare at horrible images, engage in harmful behaviour or get sucked into dangerous groups, and it will have a *significant* effect on you. No matter your age.

Some studies even show that following a big disaster on your phone can cause more lasting damage to your mental health than *actually being caught in the disaster*![48]

So yeah, your parents aren't immune to the harmful impacts of phones any more than you are.

Even if they were, some research shows that one of the best ways to reduce *your* screen time is *for parents to reduce theirs first*. It's really hard to think, 'Screens are bad for me, I should stop looking at them,' when the person telling you that is constantly staring at theirs!

48. We'll see why in a later chapter.

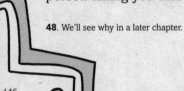

'THAT'S A GOOD POINT. IF MY PARENTS THINK PHONES ARE SO BAD, WHY DO THEY USE THEM AT *ALL*?'

Well, with parents, there's a difference between 'bad for my kids' and 'bad for *me*'.

A lot of adult life involves doing things that are bad for you. Whether it's drinking alcohol, smoking, eating fatty foods, playing dangerous sports, driving fast cars . . . Part of being an adult is getting to look at the downsides of doing something enjoyable and saying, 'You know what? I'm OK with that.'[49]

You'd be surprised how often this happens. For example, some of the biggest smokers and drinkers you'll meet are often doctors and medical staff, people who know how harmful those things are more than anyone. But they also have incredibly stressful jobs, so have more need for things that make them feel better and calmer, even briefly.

This isn't automatically a *good* thing, obviously.

---

49. There's a lot of complex brain stuff around this, which we'll be delving into a bit soon enough.

Regularly indulging in things that are bad for you, even for 'good' reasons, can quickly lead to harmful consequences (alcohol dependence, addiction, weight gain and poor health are some).

What it boils down to is that *your* well-being and health is your *parents'* responsibility. While your parents' well-being is . . . *also* your parents' responsibility. And most parents will value *your* well-being more than their own. Which is nice, when you think about it.

But also annoying.

'IS THAT WHY MY PARENTS TELL ME OFF FOR DOING STUFF THAT *THEY* DO?'

Yeah, that's a thing, isn't it?

And it's not just about phones. Many parents will firmly tell you not to drink or smoke because it's bad for you, but still happily light up a cigarette or spend hours in the pub at weekends, staggering home well after midnight.

You may have even heard your parents telling stories about how they'd do things that their parents (your grandparents) told them not to. But if *you* do the same, apparently it's the end of the world! And parents wonder why you get so mad at them, so often?

But it usually comes down to the same reason. Thanks to how our brains work, it's actually much easier to take risks and break rules when it's just *your own* well-being that matters. If it's other people's, it's much harder.

Have you ever heard it said that it's much easier to give advice to other people than it is to follow that advice yourself?[50] If you haven't . . . well, it's true.

Especially when those 'other people' are your children. The protective instinct parents have towards their offspring can be one of the deepest and most powerful of any mammal.[51]

---

50. It's a bit like a psychic predicting lottery numbers. Like, mate, if you know what the lottery numbers are going to be, why aren't *you* a millionaire?

51. Specifically, mammals. And maybe some birds. For most other species, the parent gives birth and it's like, 'Nice to meet you, kid, good luck out there,' before running off.

Of course, in other species, it can mean mothers fighting off scary predators twice their size.

In humans, it can mean parents saying:

'I'M NOT 100 PER CENT SURE A PHONE IS SAFE FOR YOU, SO YOU CAN'T HAVE ONE . . . BUT I CAN.'

Which is frustrating, from your perspective.

That's a key word: your *perspective*. We just have so much *more* to think about when it comes to our own life and decisions. We have access to all our memories and feelings and experiences. We don't have that with other people, no matter how close we are to them.

This means that giving advice and making decisions for other people can be as easy as pointing them in a certain direction when they're lost. We aren't distracted by all the internal thoughts and memories and doubts that are probably holding them back. This happens with many people, *especially* parents with their kids, because they're much more invested in them being the best they can be.

But making changes for *ourselves*? That can be like trying to make a cruise ship do a U-turn.

And, obviously, you and your parents will have very different perspectives about what's safe and important, particularly when it comes to phones. To them, it'll look like you're being disrespectful, disobedient and all sorts of other bad things if you use your phone more than they tell you to. And if they feel your phone is somehow harming you, the parental protective instinct will kick in too.

For you, it'll look like they're being massive hypocrites: they give you rules about your phone, but never follow them for theirs.

In truth, there are valid reasons and points for both points of view.

It just doesn't lead to easy conversations.

'IT WOULD BE EASIER IF MY PARENTS DIDN'T KEEP *CHANGING* THEIR RULES.'

Ah, now there's a thing.

I visited several schools while writing this book and spoke to the kids there. And one frequent complaint from students was that they had brothers or sisters who had different rules about phones than they did.

I mean, how could that not be annoying?[52]

The interesting part, though, was how everyone had a *different* experience of this. But they were *all* frustrating. Maybe you can relate?

52. Some might say that 'having brothers or sisters' is annoying enough by itself. And they'd be right.

If you're the eldest sibling and your parents have *looser* rules about phones for your younger siblings, giving them more freedom to do what they want with their devices . . .

WHAT THE HELL?

SPOILING THE LITTLE BRATS AGAIN!

That's just how brother/sister relationships work when you're young. There's almost *always* a competitive thing going on. And how your parents treat you can fuel it.

But . . . what are your parents meant to do? They honestly can't win.

You might think they should impose the exact same rules on you as your younger/older siblings. But remember what we discussed about development and milestones? These are big deals when you're younger. Expect an 11-year-old and a 16-year-old to do the exact same things and follow the exact same rules? That would be ludicrous.

And where would it end? You have to wear the same size clothes? Do the same activities? Have the same friends? That would just wind everyone up!

Unfortunately, *equality* **is not the same as *fairness*.**

And treating you and your siblings the *exact* same wouldn't be fair on anyone.

'BUT WHY DO PARENTS KEEP CHANGING THE RULES AND THEIR MINDS?'

Good point.

Shouldn't a younger sibling have the same rules about phones when they're, let's say ten, as the oldest child had when *they* were ten?

Yes, but believe it or not, every parent is still figuring things out as they go along. A parent could read every single parenting guide ever written, but nobody's ever had *their* exact kid(s) in *their* exact situation. So every parent is essentially 'learning on the job'.

Which means they'll maybe think, 'We gave [older child] a phone with *these* rules at *this* age and got *these* results. If we give [younger child] *different* rules, at the same age, we could get *different* results. And they might be better . . .'

This doesn't automatically mean the eldest is a 'practice' child or anything like that. But if you've gone through the whole phone issue with one child, it would be weird if that didn't affect your decisions when doing it again with another child.

And don't forget, technology itself keeps changing, and changing fast. A phone *now* is different to one from five years ago. And a phone five years from now will differ from one today.

Parents, with all their responsibilities and ageing brains, are doing well if they can keep up with this *at all*. And if they change their minds about stuff . . . that's actually a *good* thing.

'IT'S . . . *GOOD* IF MY PARENTS KEEP CHANGING THEIR MINDS ABOUT PHONES?'

Yes. Well, it *can* be. I guess if they're going from super-strict to 'I don't care at all' every two hours that would be bad.

But in general – whether it's the 'things were better in MY day!' brigade or being unable to appreciate that their once helpless child is growing up and becoming an independent person – it's when parents *can't* or *won't* change their minds that problems arise.

Like I say, parents are figuring things out as they go along. Especially when it comes to phones and tech, stuff they didn't grow up with.

At the end of the day, both you, their child, and the world around them is constantly changing. And while them changing their minds can be really, *really* annoying, you should actually *want* your parents to at least try to alter their thinking along with it.

Because they'll never learn otherwise, and learning is important.

CHAPTER 3

'WHO ARE YOU TALKING TO?'

OK, so we've looked at how your phone affects you, in terms of health and well-being. Or how it *doesn't* affect you, but parents say it does. Because . . . 'parents', I guess.

We've also looked at *why* your parents, with their outdated adult brains, have issues with your phone – and *what you do with it*.

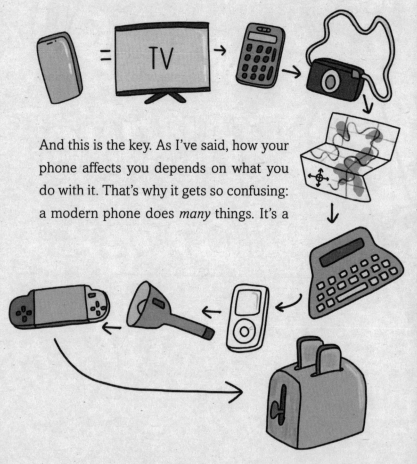

And this is the key. As I've said, how your phone affects you depends on what you do with it. That's why it gets so confusing: a modern phone does *many* things. It's a

TV, calculator, camera, map, word processor, translator, music player, torch, gaming system and, I don't know . . . a toaster?[53]

And that's before we consider that your phone has access to the internet, which contains . . . everything, ever.

However, there's one thing that *all* phones do that we *all* use them for: *communication*. Our phones allow us to reach out and connect with other people on a scale never seen before in human history. Which is cool, right?

Well, not according to your parents. Many of their complaints about your phone involve you using it to communicate with others.

Are they right to be concerned?

Well, let's see.

53. I mean, wouldn't that severely drain the battery?

'STOP BEING SO UNSOCIABLE!'

The first phones, in the 1800s, were basically wooden boxes filled with circuits, which sent very crackly voice calls to other phones through physical wires.

HELLO, IS ANYBODY THERE?

This might not sound impressive, but it was *revolutionary*. For the first time ever, people could have actual conversations over long distances.

Fast forward to the present day. Phones are now . . . a bit more complex. But even so, most of what we use them for is still to talk to people. Snapchatting, WhatsApping, posting on social media or YouTube, FaceTiming, sharing files, multiplayer gaming, working on shared documents – it's *all* some form of communication.

Some studies suggest that at least half the time you spend using your phone involves communicating with others in some way.

In fact, when we looked at what age you should be to get a phone, we discovered that, despite all their complaints, there are situations when your parents *want you to have a phone* because they *want to communicate with you*. Phones allow them to do this.

But, for some bizarre reason, if you use your phone a lot, you parents will often complain you're being *anti*social.

'YES! MY PARENTS DO SAY THAT SPENDING TOO LONG ON MY PHONE IS *ANTISOCIAL*! WHAT'S THAT ABOUT?'

Right? You're using your phone to talk to lots of people, and your parents think you're being *anti*social? Surely that's wrong.

Well, it is wrong, in the sense that it's the wrong word. Antisocial describes when someone *deliberately* breaks rules or laws to make other people miserable.

If you walked into your front room and started swearing at everyone, set fire to the sofa and threw the cat out of the window so you could record your parents' horrified reaction for TikTok . . . *that* would be an antisocial use of your phone.

But sitting quietly and using your phone without bothering anyone? That's not antisocial. The word your parents are looking for is 'unsociable'. Which means being reluctant to interact and generally not engaging with others – talking to them, sharing stories, laughing about old times, gossiping about friends and family, etc.

'OK, FINE. ARE MY PARENTS RIGHT TO SAY I'M *UNSOCIABLE* IF I USE MY PHONE TOO MUCH?'

That's where it gets tricky. If there's nobody around to talk to, using your phone to chat with people makes you *more* social, not less. Without it, you'd just be talking out loud – to no one. People think you're a bit weird if you do that.

But if there *are* others about, like parents and family, and you focus on your phone rather than them, that can *seem* unsociable. To those around you.

But . . . you are still talking to people, interacting with them – you are still socializing. You're just doing it with your phone, not in person. Some people prefer that. Others don't. Your parents are usually the second one. And so we get disagreements and conflict about whether or not you're being sociable.

'BUT WHY DO MY PARENTS CARE ABOUT ME SOCIALIZING SO MUCH IN THE FIRST PLACE?'

Ah, *now* it gets interesting.

Parents do get worked up about you socializing *in person*, don't they? Whenever there's someone in your house, they'll insist that you at least say hello. Even if it's someone like your grandparents, who you've seen countless times and will definitely see again. Will they somehow forget you exist if you skip a hello? Are your parents getting paid per brief greeting? What's the big deal?

But here's the thing: it *is* a big deal.

Being sociable is a **_vital_ part of being human**.

'SAYING HELLO TO MY GRAN FOR THE MILLIONTH TIME IS *THAT* IMPORTANT?'

Yes!

Well, no, not *specifically* that. But, in general, being social is a crucial part of being human.

There are many species of animal that are classed as 'social' because they live in large groups and generally work together. Rats and other rodents, wolf packs, lion prides, primates of all types: they're all social.

But humans . . . we go even further. We're what's known as *ultra* social. Which means that, really, we're the most tolerant, friendly species that's ever lived.

'THAT CAN'T BE RIGHT. JUST LOOK AT THE NEWS OR THE FACT THAT PEOPLE ARE HORRIBLE TO EACH OTHER ONLINE. PEOPLE ARE REALLY *INTOLERANT*!'

I get your point. But that's not how it works.

Sure, many people can be 'toxic', as they say. But on average, humans are still better at *putting up with each other* than any other species. Our biggest cities are more crowded than the typical ant colony!

In fact, the species we're most closely related to, chimpanzees, aren't anywhere near as tolerant of each other as us.

You have assemblies in school, right? Where hundreds of you end up packed into the main school hall to listen to your headteacher or whoever droning on about things they think you should care about.

But if everyone in the assembly halls was suddenly transformed into a chimp, it would turn into an absolute bloodbath. The walls would be splattered with banana and poo.

Despite being 98.8 per cent human,[54] chimps are *much* less friendly and *much* less tolerant of each other than we are. We rarely have any issue with being packed in with dozens, hundreds, *thousands* of other humans. Sometimes we actually *enjoy* it. That's why stadiums exist.

But put too many chimps in an enclosed space and they'll totally freak out. Half of them would be dead within minutes. The other half would be eating them.[55]

'I DON'T THINK MY PARENTS ARE WORRIED THAT MY PHONE IS GOING TO MAKE ME START EATING PEOPLE.'

Probably not, no.

But compared to most species, humans are *very* friendly and tolerant. Our interactions and relationships with others, being *sociable*, is important to us.

54. Humans and chimps evolved from the same species in the distant past. It's like both species share the same great-great-great-great-great-great-great-great-great-great-great-great-great-great-grandparents. And so our DNA is very similar.
55. It's true. Chimps often turn cannibal and eat their fallen enemies. Why? Nobody is sure.

Much of your brain is dedicated to **socializing and forming connections with other people.**

Our brains often *depend* on our interactions with others to do what they do. Keeping people away from other humans is recognized as actual *torture*. It's like having your legs broken, then trying to run a 5K: everything becomes more difficult and unpleasant.

Basically, we humans *need* to socialize.[56]

That might be why your parents think being sociable is so important. *It is.*

'*WHY* IS BEING SOCIABLE SO IMPORTANT?'

Valid question. After all, it's not like air. We won't collapse to the floor, gasping, if we go several minutes

---

56. Although that doesn't automatically mean we need to constantly socialize with *everyone*. We need to eat too, but we don't need to eat all food all the time.

without chatting about the weather or sharing a meme.

However, being sociable has always been very important for humans as a *species*.

Basically, humans aren't the strongest, fastest or biggest animal. We don't have claws, fangs, armour or other cool weapons or defences. We can't fly or swim that well. Compared to more impressive creatures, we're just a load of shambling organs wrapped in soft skin. Doesn't sound like something that would rule the planet.

But we do. And the secret of our success (it's believed by clever scientists) is how friendly and tolerant we are with each other.

Think about it: the more friendly and cooperative early humans were, the more likely they were to survive and thrive. A bear or sabre-toothed tiger could easily take out a human one-on-one. But five humans? Ten? *Fifty?* All *working together*? Fat chance, Pooh and Tigger.

Close groups of humans could also look after the injured and vulnerable, defend the tribe, share useful information (like where the best berries are) and so on.

However, things like forming relationships, making plans, sharing information . . . these are all very complex mental abilities. To do these things well, you're going to need a lot of brain power. Many scientists now believe that the human brain is as smart and powerful as it is because it *needed* to be to keep up with all the relationships and interactions that kept us alive.

And so we end up with a human brain that is dedicated to, and often dependant on, cooperation, friendship, *socializing*. It's the secret to our success.

'I THOUGHT IT WAS ALL "SURVIVAL OF THE FITTEST", "DOG EAT DOG"?'

Nah, that's an old-fashioned idea. Cooperating and friendliness is a vital part of human success. Anyone who says otherwise is either a nineteenth-century biologist or someone trying to justify being a bully.

'BUT IF BEING SOCIABLE IS SO IMPORTANT . . . WHY'S IT SO STRESSFUL?'

Bingo!

Because it really can be. *Especially* when you're younger, going through your teens. Having long conversations with people can be exhausting. Large crowds can be overwhelming. Asking someone out, romantically, can be absolutely terrifying.[57]

This doesn't necessarily change when you're an adult, when your emotions are said to have 'settled down'. Countless people are just shy. You might have heard of extroverts and introverts – introverts are essentially people who don't particularly like or enjoy socializing or interacting with people (that they don't already know).[58]

---

57. I had my first girlfriend when I was 18. And *she* asked *me* out. So yeah, I found it scary.
58. For the record, there's absolutely nothing wrong with this. Humans vary. It's fine.

'DOESN'T THIS FLY IN THE FACE OF THE WHOLE "BEING SOCIABLE IS VITAL" THING?'

No.

While socializing is important, it's still *work*. For your brain, I mean. Interacting with other people takes a lot of brain power. That's why even the most outgoing, bubbly extrovert needs some quiet time eventually.

Humans may need to socialize, but they also need privacy, **to rest and recharge**.

That's why it's also important to have your own space. If your parents or siblings are the sort to just wander into your room without asking, you know how stressful it is even if they mean no harm.[59] So not all socializing and interacting is automatically good.

---

59. Although there's a good chance your younger siblings are genuinely trying to annoy you.

'BEING SOCIABLE IS HARD BECAUSE IT'S SOMETIMES TOO MUCH WORK FOR OUR BRAINS?'

Yes. But it's not *just* that.

Sociability (basically, 'being social') is very important for our brains. So much so that a positive social interaction, even if it's a brief one, like a stranger saying 'thanks' for you holding the door open for them, causes our brains to experience pleasure.

But the downside of this is that our brains are very sensitive to rejection. Say you want to join in someone's game or just say hello, because you're in a new place and don't know anyone. So you go and say 'hi' to someone with these things in mind, and they . . . just say no. Or don't respond at all. Anyone who's experienced this will know it's *really* uncomfortable.

These are actually very mild examples of *failed* socialization, not making a connection. Our brains really dislike that. Scientific studies have revealed that being rejected by others, even complete strangers, even if *you don't really mind if they don't like you*, causes emotional pain.

This means that every time you socialize with someone and keep up with what they are saying and doing, and all the mental work that involves, your brain is constantly trying to present the best possible version of yourself. This is to avoid embarrassment, avoid offending the other person and to avoid being rejected.

Overall, socializing is always a bit of a gamble. The pleasure and reward of making friends and bonding versus the risk of rejection and criticism.

And some people have brains that focus more on the risk than the reward. Which is probably why we have introverts.

'THAT ALL SOUNDS EXHAUSTING. WOULDN'T IT BE EASIER TO JUST USE MY PHONE TO INTERACT?'

You've basically hit the nail on the head.

Communicating and socializing via your phone or device is **much *easier*, as far as your brain is concerned, than doing it in person**.

You've much more control over how others see you, and far more time to consider your replies and reactions. You can speak to many people at once, without having to raise your voice or even get up. And if you *do* say or do something wrong or embarrassing, you have more options for doing something about it. You can't delete an accidental insult if you've said it aloud.

It's just easier all round, isn't it? Communicating with a phone – something that is literally designed for communicating – takes a lot of pressure off your brain.[60]

'WHY DON'T MY PARENTS THINK LIKE THAT?'

Good point. Clearly, your parents think socializing in person is more important, and better, than doing it with your phone.

This will partly be an age thing. Remember, they didn't grow up with phones, so to them, and other adults, socializing with phones isn't 'proper' socializing. The concept is still new and unfamiliar to them.

Also, socializing with the phone doesn't *look* like socializing from the outside. Unless you're the one using the phone, chatting with dozens of people looks exactly like playing games or watching YouTube.

---

60. This may explain why neurodivergent people – those with autism, for instance – often prefer to communicate through screens and devices. Screen communication is much more ordered, logical and controlled. Just what you need if you've the sort of brain that finds other people confusing sometimes.

Also, if you're focusing on the conversations happening via your phone, rather than responding to the people physically in front of you trying to talk to you, it seems like you're ignoring them. It looks rude.

And many parents would say you *are* ignoring them, so you *are* being rude. And maybe they have a point.

But it's not that simple. Basically, your brain has a choice: respond to the person right in front of you or the people in your phone. For your brain, the second option is a lot easier, probably more entertaining and less 'risky'. So obviously, you'll lean towards that choice.

Your parents maybe wouldn't make the same decision. But then, they, with their older brains, see the world very differently to you. That's why you end up arguing about it a lot.

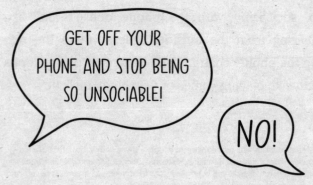

GET OFF YOUR PHONE AND STOP BEING SO UNSOCIABLE!

NO!

'MY PARENTS THINK SOCIALIZING IN PERSON IS BETTER THAN DOING IT WITH YOUR PHONE. IS THAT TRUE?'

OK, so the thing about that is . . .

Actually, you know what? This is such a good question it deserves its own section.

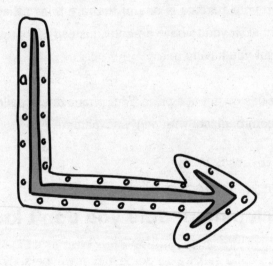

'THEY'RE NOT ACTUALLY YOUR FRIENDS.'

So phones let you communicate. In fact, communicating with your parents is one of the rare things that mean they *want* you to have a phone, instead of just whining about you having one.

But this comes at a price. Your phone doesn't allow you to communicate with *only* your parents. No.

It allows you to communicate with anyone. **Including people you don't know.**

Your child talking to some unknown person? Every parent is concerned about this exact thing. So if you spend hours on your phone talking to people your parents have no clue about rather than interacting with friends in the 'real world', this can seem 'unhealthy'.

Because you're staying indoors rather than going outside. You're not doing 'proper' face-to-face interacting and your parents don't really know *who* you're talking to on your phone.

But at least *you* know, right?

. . . Right?

'UH . . . YES? I *DO* KNOW WHO I'M TALKING TO ON MY PHONE.'

Well, yes. At your age, the contacts in your phone will likely be people you already know. Why would you have their number if you didn't know them?

It's different for parents. They're *always* talking to people they don't know. Customers, shop assistants, salespeople, bank clerks, delivery services, mechanics, waiting staff. The number of times you have to communicate with a complete stranger as an adult is off the scale.

THANK YOU FOR CALLING THE WATER COMPANY, HOW MAY I HELP YOU?

YEAH, MY TOILET JUST EXPLODED. CAN YOU SEND SOMEONE TO FIX IT? IT'S PRETTY URGENT.

Phones have made this *ten times worse*. Now anybody with your contact details can 'get in touch', whenever they like, from anywhere, for any reason.

Life is weird for modern parents. Their whole childhood, they were told:

NEVER SPEAK TO STRANGERS!

Then they grew up and now they have to speak to strangers all the time! And then everyone got a phone, which is basically a 'speaking to strangers' machine.

And now you, their child, have your own phone! And it's possible for you to speak to strangers, and for them to get in touch with you, for whatever dodgy reason, without your parents even realizing it's happening. You can see why they might be a bit worried.

'OK. BUT AGAIN . . . I *DON'T* SPEAK TO STRANGERS. EVERYONE I SPEAK TO IS SOMEONE I KNOW.'

Sure. But do you *actually* know everyone you're talking to with your phone? Or do you just *know who they are*?

'I-I DON'T . . . WHAT'S THE DIFFERENCE?'

Look at it this way: I know who Taylor Swift is.

But do I *know* Taylor Swift? Like, personally? No. If I tried to wander into her house, I'd be immediately arrested. But someone doesn't need to be a superstar for you to know of, but not 'know', them.

When my son started at secondary school, he was added to a group chat for all the other new students starting that year. Which is nice. But it's a big school, so the group chat included about 200 kids.

For most of these kids, my son knew *who they were*. He could say:

OH, THAT'S VERITY BOOGLESNAP, SHE'S IN CLASS 2B.[61]

But despite being in the group chat, was he *good friends* with all these students?

No. Not because he's rude or unsociable. But, being proper friends, with 200 people, in one go? That's more than our brains can deal with.

'BUT YOU SAID OUR BRAINS WERE ALL ABOUT SOCIALIZING AND MAKING FRIENDS?'

I did. And it's true. Mostly.

But that doesn't mean we have *infinite* ability to make friends. A crane is designed to lift heavy loads, but

61. To clarify, my son does *not* go to school with a Verity Booglesnap. I made the name up for a laugh. Of course if that *is* your name . . . I'm *really* sorry. For several reasons.

there'll still be things too big and heavy for the crane to lift, and it'll snap or burst into flames if it tries.

While your brain isn't going to burst into flames, its ability to make friends is limited because friendships take up a surprising amount of space in our brain. And the stronger or deeper the friendship, the more brain space it occupies. For starters, you'll spend a lot of time with a good friend. So they'll take up a lot of memory space.

But it's not just memories: a friend is someone you *think* about too. A lot.

For example, say you see a trailer for a new film and think:

> I BET MY BEST FRIEND, VERITY BOOGLESNAP, WOULD LIKE TO SEE THAT WITH ME.

While it doesn't sound like much, your brain's doing a lot of work for this simple thought.

It's absorbed the information from the trailer and checked it against everything you know about your best mate, Verity. Including how much money she has, her schedule, other films she's seen and how much you think she'd like to see it.

This takes up a lot of brainpower, something you only have a certain amount of. And if so much brainpower is spent thinking about Verity, there's less to go around for others.

This means our brain can only manage so many friendships before we get overwhelmed. Renowned anthropologist[62] Robin Dunbar thinks that the maximum number of relationships we can maintain is around 150.

But it's not a 'one size fits all' thing. Good, close friends like Verity? We usually only have five or six of those, at most, thanks to all the brain space they take up.

The rest of your friends can still be *good* friends, but a bit more distant. Beyond that, they're classmates, distant relatives, acquaintances, basically people you *know* but not much more than that.

---

62. Someone who studies humans and the cultures and societies they exist in.

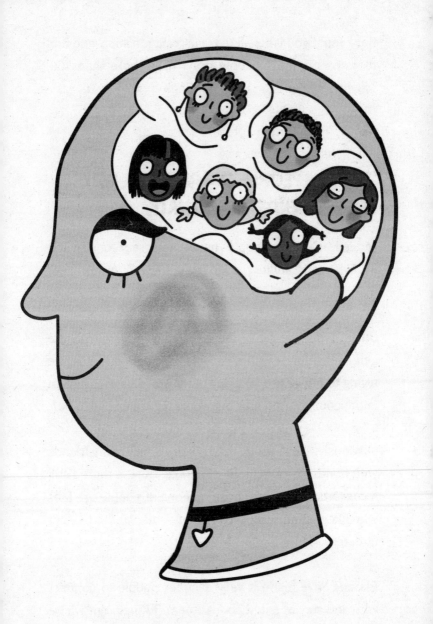

But even if you label all these as 'relationships' and add them all up, most people don't have more than 200. Maybe Dunbar is on to something?

'BUT . . . PEOPLE ONLINE HAVE *WAY MORE* FRIENDS THAN THAT!'

Indeed. Certain people have Instagram or TikTok profiles with *millions* of followers. Even *hundreds* of millions!

But . . . do you really think that those individuals are genuinely friends with *a hundred million people*? Imagine trying to organize a birthday party. You'd have to hire an entire country. And how big would the cake need to be?

Obviously, these social media stars aren't *really* friends with hundreds of millions of people. But . . . there's still a *connection*, sort of. Those millions of people are fans who like the famous person's work and want to be kept updated.

Phones have made it very easy for people to connect with and stay updated about others. To the point where one person can have hundreds of millions of people regularly checking in on what they're up to.

It sounds scary when you put it like that. No wonder parents get worried!

'IS THAT WHY WE CAN HAVE SO MANY MORE "ONLINE" FRIENDS THAN REAL-WORLD ONES? BECAUSE PHONES MAKE IT EASIER?'

Exactly!

Usually with friendships, your brain's doing all the work. But if your phone is involved, you don't *need* to remember someone's face, name, age, likes and so on. Your phone remembers it for you. Just like your parents worried about![63]

---

63. See Chapter 1. Although, it's not the same thing. Very few parents worry that your phone is 'replacing' your ability to remember 4,000 people's details. They probably don't want you doing that in the first place.

And on top of that, phones make your friends want to share fun stuff with you and others. And you with them.

Imagine wandering up to a group of your friends in the playground, shoving a painting in their faces and yelling:

> LOOK AT THIS! I MADE IT.

To do that, you'd have to be extremely confident.

Remember, rejection is a constant risk in the real world. So even if you *want* to show your friends your latest painting in person, your brain will say:

> WHAT IF THEY HATE IT SO MUCH THEY LITERALLY THROW UP?

And now you can't *not* worry about that happening, no matter how unlikely it is.

But sharing through phones and screens? There are layers of safety between you and rejection. Even if your friends *do* throw up when you post your latest painting on Instagram, you'll never see it. So you'll feel more willing to put yourself and your stuff 'out there', even though it's probably reaching way more people than if you did it in person.[64]

So yeah, phones do a lot of the heavy lifting when it comes to friendships, which allows you to maintain connections with far more people than you ever could in person. And so you end up with far more online friends.

'MAXIMUM FRIENDS, MINIMUM EFFORT? THAT SOUNDS GREAT. WHY DO MY PARENTS KEEP INSISTING I TALK TO PEOPLE IN PERSON?'

I get your point. Online communication and relationships tick so many boxes for the typical human brain. So why not just have friendships that way?

Well, look at it this way: do you eat food? I'm guessing . . . yes.

---

64. This is particularly true for young people like yourself. Your emotions tend to hit a lot harder than for your parents, and the approval of others is really important in your development. As we'll soon see.

But what if I told you there's this new super vitamin pill that meets all your body's needs? You can take that instead of all that cooking and chewing and swallowing. You'll never need to eat again!

Would you do that? Replace eating food with a convenient pill? I'm guessing . . . no.

Because we *like* eating. It's not just about fuel: eating is an enjoyable thing. If you *did* replace eating meals with a pill, you likely wouldn't be happy. And probably not that healthy, either: your digestive system is *meant* to work with multiple sources of solid food, such as fruits, vegetables, meats, grains and so on.

And if you deprive a vital organ of what it's evolved to work with, things start to go wrong.

'ARE YOU SAYING I SHOULD *EAT* MY PHONE?'

No! Why would I . . . Look, my point is, just like how your digestive system *expects* proper food, and would sorely miss it, your *brain* evolved to expect real-world interactions and friendships. And all the rich information they contain. Like body language, eye movements, physical touch, speech patterns, even a person's *smell*. Our brain uses all this stuff when we talk to someone face-to-face. So it *expects* it when we communicate.

Because it normally has all this stuff to work with, our brains think that communication and relationships in the real world are more . . . well, real.

'IS A FRIENDSHIP OR RELATIONSHIP ONLY "REAL" IF IT HAPPENS IN PERSON?'

Actually, no. It's entirely possible to connect with people entirely online through your phone. I've made many good friends purely via Twitter.[65] And I know a number of married couples with kids who got together through online dating.

So yes, online relationships can be legit.

---

65. A social media platform from the past. People would get angry on it a lot, but it was also fun at times.

However, if your best friend called you in tears about something . . . would you go to see them? Or just stay on the phone, sending reassuring messages and some funny memes?

If a beloved family member said they were moving to a different country and you'd never see them again, would you be sad? Or would you say, 'It's fine, we can stay in touch online. It's the same thing.'?

Basically, thanks to how our brains work, online friendships and relationships *can* be totally real. But the communication and socializing that happens in person will always be more *significant* and more *rewarding*.

This is because your brain thinks face-to-face communication is important. **And that's crucial.**

Remember: your relationships and interactions have a big impact on how you think and develop. And the most significant relationships will have the most impact. So the friendships and connections you have in the real world will be the most *important* in a number of ways.

'SO . . . MY PARENTS ARE RIGHT? I SHOULD SPEND MORE TIME SOCIALIZING AWAY FROM MY PHONE?'

Well . . . sort of? But only by accident. They probably don't know all the stuff I just told you, unless they're neuroscientists too.

But they may have some gut feeling that you should speak to people more in person rather than stick to your phone. Although they probably don't know *why* they think that.

Another thing they probably don't realize is that if you're not socializing in the real world enough, that's sort of their fault.

'WAIT . . . *WHAT?*'

Oh yeah. Didn't I mention that already? Well, allow me to explain . . .

'YOU KIDS ARE SO SELF-OBSESSED!'

Have you been called vain? Arrogant? Self-obsessed? Or something like that?

In fairness, it probably wasn't by your own parents. They're hopefully not *that* rude. But you've probably heard this stuff said about 'kids today' (which includes you) by those outspoken[66] adults who are always on TV or in newspapers.[67]

Because you young people are so *self-absorbed*. You're always taking selfies, making YouTube or TikTok videos of yourself, livestreaming as you talk loudly while playing video games: it's all

LOOK AT ME! LOOK AT ME!

[66]. Which is a nice way of saying 'grumpy loudmouth'.
[67]. Being accused of arrogance by someone who thinks millions of people *need* to know their opinions? Bit rich.

And it's all thanks to your phone! Phones encourage you to share everything about yourself with countless others, and it's turning you young people into arrogant monsters!

That's the accusation, anyway. And, obviously, it's wrong. For many reasons.

Why do so many adults think this, though?

'WAIT . . . YOU JUST SAID YOU'D EXPLAIN WHY NOT SOCIALIZING IN PERSON IS ACTUALLY MY PARENTS' FAULT.'

I did. I *am*.

This stuff is actually part of that.

'WEIRD! BUT OK . . . SO MY PHONE *DOESN'T* MAKE ME SELF-OBSESSED?'

Much of the time, no. It *looks* that way, to older people, but that's actually down to how modern phones work.

For example, with an in-person interaction, you're always *there*. Which means you're still involved in what's going on, even if you're totally silent.

But when interacting through phones, if you're not saying or sharing stuff, it's like you're *not* there. As far as the brain is concerned, a little profile pic with the word 'online' next to it just isn't the same. Basically, you have to constantly say 'Look at me', in some way, just to stay involved.

Some parents might say you still focus on yourself too much, on what you're doing and thinking, when interacting through your phone. But . . . what else are you meant to share on *your* profile? That's the whole point of it! If you used your profile to share pictures of your neighbour or things your seven-year-old second cousin says, everyone would think you're strange.

And if you counted all the face-to-face conversations your parents have and worked out how much they talked about their own views and opinions and experiences, I guarantee you it would be pretty high. But it's only self-obsessed if it happens on a screen? That's not exactly fair.

As for selfies, people like seeing who they're talking to. Showing others your face is *arrogant* now? Most adults would say hiding your face during a conversation was suspicious and worrying. Again, why is it different if you do it through your phone?

Basically, it probably *is* fair to say that you do share more of yourself when communicating with your phone. And it quickly becomes normal. After all, you'd probably never stand in front of dozens of people and say:

> LOOK HOW ATTRACTIVE/
> INTERESTING/FUNNY I AM!

But you're sort of doing that with your phone all the time.

But this *doesn't* mean you're self-obsessed.

'I FEEL LIKE THERE'S ANOTHER "BUT" COMING.'

Yup.

As always, there's more going on.

Think about the stuff that you create and share through your phone. How much of it is some way of saying, 'Look how funny/creative/beautiful/smart/wise/compassionate I am!' and 'Look how good I am at this thing.' If you're being honest, it's probably a lot. Whether it's jokes, beautiful photos, selfies, witty comments, sick burns, advice or video game scores.

Nothing wrong with this, by the way. We all do it.[68] But it shows that, when communicating with your phone, you're not just saying 'talk to me'. You're also often saying:

BE *IMPRESSED* BY ME!
LIKE ME!

But this isn't your phone's doing. Your brain is actually to blame. Your phone just . . . amplifies everything.

---

68. You're literally reading a book that I wrote to share my brilliance with you.

'OUR BRAINS MAKE US SUPER-FRIENDLY . . . *AND* MAKE US SHOW OFF CONSTANTLY?'

OK, it seems weird when you put it like that. Nobody sees a massive show-off and thinks, 'I need to be their friend!'

But these things aren't actually that different. Sure, our brains make us want to connect and form relationships with others, but that's a lot easier if we're *liked* by others. Respected. Looked up to. Admired.

Basically, our brains really care about **social status**.

'SOCIAL STATUS? IS THAT TO DO WITH SOCIAL MEDIA?'

Not exactly. It's been a thing for millions of years, so a bit before social media. Social status is basically your 'value' or 'rank' compared to the other people in your group or community.

For instance, you might be one of many students hoping to get into the school netball team. If you do eventually make the team, you'd be 'higher status' than those who didn't. But if you're then dropped and replaced by someone else, you'd be lower status than *that* person.

That's just one (*very* simple) example of social status, which is basically the human tendency to look around at others and think, 'Who is above me, and who is below me?'

'ISN'T THAT JUST POPULARITY?'

Yes! Popularity is a form of social status. But there are others and they can all affect us.

'BUT WE'RE ALWAYS TOLD TO NOT CARE ABOUT BEING POPULAR. TO BE OURSELVES. STUFF LIKE THAT.'

Yeah, that's a tricky one.

It *is* better for you not to compare yourself to others. But the deeper, older parts of your brain, the parts that do their own thing without you knowing, they *do* care about social status. A lot.

Basically, it's human nature to want at least *some* people to look up to us.[69] Which explains why the higher our social status, the happier we tend to be.

On the flip side, if our status goes *down*, we really *don't* like that.

Remember how our brains experience pleasure from acceptance and pain from rejection? **This is another form of that**.

---

69. *Especially* for younger brains, which are most sensitive to this urge.

'WHY IS SOCIAL STATUS SUCH A BIG DEAL?'

Many reasons. For example, having lots of people respect and admire you, is like having layers of armour between yourself and painful rejection. It makes it easier to ignore 'the haters'.[70]

Meanwhile, being very *low* status means, whatever you do, you experience rejection all the time. That's *very* stressful. Like your brain is walking barefoot over a field of Lego pieces and dog muck. That's why low social status is strongly linked to mental health problems.

'THAT'S ROUGH! CAN WE AVOID THAT BY *INCREASING* OUR STATUS?'

You *can*. The question is, *how*? How do you make lots of people like and respect you?

You might think that's an easy question, but it can't be. If everyone can easily increase their social status, it becomes meaningless.

70. Or is that 'h8ers'?

When everyone's a winner . . .
nobody is.

We humans are very complicated. So is the world we live in. This means social status can be achieved by *many* different things.

For example, popularity is a type of social status, like you said. And I'm guessing your school, if it's like every school ever, has students who are 'the popular ones'.[71]

'YES.'

But *why* are they the most popular?

'ERM . . . LOTS OF REASONS?'

Exactly.

---

71. Doesn't matter if that applies to you or not, so I won't ask.

Maybe they're the best looking, richest, most fashionable, sportiest, funniest or something even harder to pin down, like 'coolest'. There are many ways to become popular.

But none of these things *guarantee* popularity. For example, you could be the richest kid in school, but saying 'I'm richer than you!' to everyone *won't* make you popular, even if it's true. There are many ways to be *un*popular too.

Also, what makes someone popular is always changing. Like fashion.

Fashion's a perfect example. When I was in school, the 'cool' boys wore shellsuits[72] and had blonde, spiked hair. But if someone from your school turned up looking like that now, how long would it be before everyone stopped laughing?

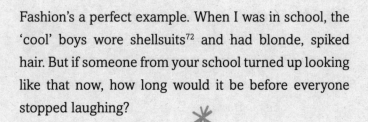

Also, when I was young, guys who constantly played video games were seen as massive losers. Now? They're

---

72. If you don't know what a 'shellsuit' is, I urge you to look it up. Yes, we used to wear them. No, not as a joke.

polishing Lamborghinis with £50 notes, thanks to all the money they make from popular YouTube channels.[73]

Overall, the only thing that's guaranteed to make you popular (high status) is . . . everyone agreeing that you are.

'IT'S SO CONFUSING! IS SOCIAL STATUS WORTH ALL THIS BOTHER?'

It can be hard work, sure. Luckily, the parts of your brain that care about status can be kept quiet just by being liked and respected by your personal friend group. That's often enough for most people.

But social status can be like food or money: you can have *enough*, but that doesn't mean you'll turn down *more*. That's why, if we get the opportunity to be liked, admired or respected by even more people (like the chance to be on TV or win a big award), it's *extremely* tempting.

---

73. I'm a fan of Typical Gamer, TG, myself. Good old Andre.

And by linking you to more people than ever before, your phone is *constantly* giving you the opportunity to raise your social status by impressing others.

'IS THAT ANOTHER REASON WHY OUR PHONE ACTIVITY CAN SEEM SELF-OBSESSED?'

Partly, yes. But it's not just that.

Wanting to be high status or popular is a powerful urge. But . . . how do we *know* for sure, how many people like and respect us?

How do we know if our efforts to impress were successful?

How can we know what people are into right now?

There's so much uncertainty around social status. Our brains don't like uncertainty. It stresses them out.

But phones? They make everything *much* clearer and easier.

Your brain doesn't wonder, 'Does anyone actually like this post?' if it has exactly 147 likes.

Sharing a funny meme in a group chat and getting countless thumbs-up and laugh emojis is much easier, and safer, than cracking jokes in person. A joke not landing in person is a special kind of awkward hell.

Posting a selfie and getting multiple heart reactions and 'Wow! Gorgeous hon' comments is much more rewarding than spending hours on your make-up and having nobody glance at you twice.

Basically, phones make you seem 'self-obsessed' because your brain craves approval from others. Phones make this much easier to get . . . but you still need to provide something for people to approve *of.* So you end up regularly sharing stuff about how great you are.

'I GUESS THAT'S ANOTHER REASON MY PARENTS THINK MY PHONE IS BAD FOR ME.'

Probably, yeah. They think it's making you self-obsessed, inconsiderate of others, just generally shallow.

But there's also another big factor at work: your *parents'* social status.

'MY PARENTS CARE ABOUT SOCIAL STATUS TOO?'

Absolutely. Social status is for life, not just for your youth.

But remember, social status can be based on *anything*, if enough people agree it's good.

Becoming a parent, for instance, is a *huge* deal. Many consider it the most important thing an adult will ever do. Parents normally need, and want, approval from other parents, to be reassured they're 'doing it' right.

So, for parents, having other parents think you're a good parent becomes very important to social status.

Seriously, it gets intense. You may think you and your friends get nasty during arguments, but you've got *nothing* on the comments on any popular 'mommy blog'. It's terrifying!

This is all because any decent parent's main concern is the safety and well-being of their children. So, to be the best possible parent (and have high social status), you need to protect your children from harm as much as possible. It's just that many parents disagree, strongly, about what is the best way to do that. So they argue. *A lot.*

However, what's the one thing that most modern parents all agree is a danger to children?

'PHONES!'

Bingo!

But in terms of social status, this causes a problem. *Your* social status depends on using your phone as much as possible. Your *parents'* social status depends on keeping you *away* from phones as much as possible.

So, with regards to phones, you and your parents have status-obsessed brains that are pulling in completely opposite directions.

Is it any wonder you argue about them so much?

'THAT'S CLEARLY GOING TO CAUSE PROBLEMS.'

It *has* caused problems. 'Keeping your child safe' was important to parents long before smartphones, and it's also been important to parents' social status that whole time. Which has changed parenting itself.

You remember how parents and older adults always moan about how, in *their* day, they'd play outside and walk everywhere? Well, what changed? Why did young people stop doing that?

Many parents blame phones and devices. But according to research, both the average time children spend outdoors, and the distance they wander from home, has been falling since the 1970s. Again, long before mobile phones were a thing.

So if phones aren't the reason for young people being indoors more, what is?

Well, there are more buildings, roads and cars around now, filling the open spaces where young people in the past would wander about.

However, the main reason young people stopped going outside so much? Their parents wouldn't let them! Year after year, parents clocked their children wandering around outdoors, out of their sight, and said:

NO! TOO DANGEROUS!

and made them stick closer to home.

Closer and closer and closer.

That's why modern young people don't socialize outdoors as much as their parents did. *Their parents stop them!*

'*THAT'S* WHY IT'S MY PARENTS' FAULT!'

Yup. Because they want to keep you as safe as possible, for the most part. But also, they want to earn the approval of other parents – which means being the best parent possible, which often means keeping your child as safe as possible. And so, your parents stop you from doing things like going to your friends house. Something you *want* to do, that they think is 'healthy'. All to keep you 'safe'. And then they blame you for being indoors too much.

And parents insist they're the *sensible* ones?

'IF THIS CARRIES ON, WON'T YOUNG PEOPLE EVENTUALLY BE STUCK INDOORS FOREVER?'

Actually, there's good news there.

Recent data suggest modern parents have started letting their children spend longer outdoors and wander further from home than in previous decades. The trend is now *reversing*. Something has changed recently.

And that something is . . . **phones**!

'WHAT?'

Yeah. Your parents are more willing to let you go out and do stuff than parents from the recent past. Because you have a phone.

Maybe they think spending all day indoors staring at your phone is more worrying than letting you out of their sight for five minutes. But a more likely explanation is that you have a phone, so you're technically *not* out of sight. Wherever and whenever you go, your phone means your parents can still know where you are and immediately get in touch.

So, overall, phones affect social status in many ways. And one of these is they've *increased* your ability to explore the real world and interact with real people face-to-face. The exact opposite of what many parents believe.

Because a phone means you're 'safe' – and so is their status as **a good parent.**

'EXACTLY! MY PARENTS WORRY ABOUT MY PHONE FOR NO REASON!'

Ah. Well. Not exactly . . .

'THEY'RE A BAD INFLUENCE!'

So, one thing is clear: your phone makes a big difference to how you interact with your family and friends.

But your phone does more than that. It allows you to interact with people you *don't* know. People you've never met. And when you consider that the group 'People you know' is made of a couple of hundred (at most), while 'People you *don't* know' is over seven *billion*, this makes it a big deal. Thanks to your phone, all those people can now *influence* you.

And that's something parents are wary of.

'ARE YOU TALKING ABOUT "INFLUENCERS"?'

I wasn't, actually. But that's a perfect place to start. Influencers! A great example of how phones affect us, thanks to our brain's obsession with interaction and status.

After all, influence means 'the power to affect how people think, behave or develop'. So young people being influenced by others, particularly in unhelpful or harmful ways, is an issue. And parents have been getting furious at the *possibility* of their children being exposed to 'bad influences' for many years.

Let me be honest. A lot of the problems parents and other adults, particularly middle-aged ones (like me), have with the whole 'influencer' thing is that it just confuses us.

For instance, to us older types, if someone says:

I'M AN INFLUENCER,

it's like asking someone what they do for a living, and they say:

I'M A MONEY EARNER.

I mean, it's technically correct, but . . . can you be a bit more specific?

Don't get me wrong, certain people having a great deal of influence and popularity is not a new thing. Whether it's movie stars, athletes, musicians, authors, composers, religious figures . . . certain people have had influence over countless others for *thousands* of years.

It's just that, all those people were popular and influential *for a specific reason*. They did something – achieved something – that made people love and admire them and so be influenced by them.

Influencers, though? They seem to just . . . exist? And loads of people love them for it. It's surreal.

'INFLUENCERS DON'T JUST "EXIST"; THERE'S MORE TO IT THAN THAT.'

Fair enough. *Everyone* exists. But not everyone's an influencer.

In my experience, when most people say 'influencer', they often mean glamorous and beautiful or otherwise impressive people. The sort that others look at and think:

I WANT TO BE
LIKE THEM!

Again, people like that have always been around. It's just, in the past, for such people to be seen by large audiences, they needed to be on TV or in magazines or something like that. And that was (and still is) hard to do; there's only so much TV and magazine space to go around. So, to make the cut, you had to be talented or otherwise 'special' in a way that people were interested in. You couldn't *just* be good looking and glamorous. At least, not at first.

Imagine trying to be an influencer *before* phones. Going up to random strangers in the supermarket with a handful of photos and saying:

WANT TO SEE THESE
PICTURES OF ME ON A BEACH?
I'M VERY ATTRACTIVE!

The general reaction would be less

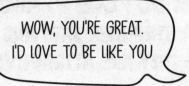

and more

GET AWAY FROM ME,
YOU MASSIVE WEIRDO!

But that's not true any more. Thanks to phones, and sites like Instagram or TikTok, you can now share your good looks, hot body, travel adventures or interesting ideas with countless people. Without needing anyone's permission or having to follow instructions or rules.

So people do. And others see them, like them, follow them, end up being influenced by them. So now we have influencers.

Maybe this is actually more *honest* than what came before. Fact is, we *like* seeing beautiful, attractive people.

'LOOKING AT THEM IS ONE THING, BUT WHY DO I *CARE* SO MUCH ABOUT WHAT A STRANGER SAYS AND DOES? EVEN IF THEY ARE ATTRACTIVE.'

Because there's a big difference between a total stranger and someone you know about but *haven't met*. Yet. Often thanks to our phones, we can know *everything* about someone without ever meeting them. Especially if they're keen on sharing their lives with others (like influencers usually do).

That can be more than enough for our brains, for us, to consider them a friend. Even though they don't know we exist.

'HOW CAN YOU BE FRIENDS WITH SOMEONE WHO DOESN'T KNOW YOU EXIST?'

Sounds ludicrous, I know. But remember earlier, when I explained how our actual friendships require a lot of brainpower? Our brain has to consider what they'd do, think or feel about things.

What I'm getting at is actual friendships involve our brains constantly *making stuff up*. The mental representation of friends held in our brains is as much a part of our friendship as the real-life person.

But to create this mental representation, we technically *don't need* to have met someone.

Basically, all our brains need to consider someone a friend, and form emotional connections with them, is enough information about them.

And today it's often *easier* to find information about your favourite celebrity than about someone who sits next to you in class. Jenny from geography lessons presumably doesn't have ten million fan pages dedicated to her.

'BUT SURELY IT'S NOT A REAL RELATIONSHIP IF ONLY ONE OF US KNOWS THE OTHER EXISTS?'

100 per cent correct.

It's a bit tricky to consider it a real friendship when one person doesn't even know the other is there. It's a bit one-sided, wouldn't you say? That's why this sort of thing is called a **parasocial** relationship.

And thanks to phones, parasocial relationships are more common than ever.

'IS THAT WHY OUR PARENTS DON'T LIKE OUR PHONES? THEY MAKE US CARE SO MUCH ABOUT PEOPLE WE'VE NEVER MET AND WHO DON'T KNOW US?'

Your parents might feel that way, but it would be unfair. Because parasocial relationships have been around much longer than phones.

Given your age, I'm guessing you've had a crush on someone at some point? If you haven't, just . . . give it time. I only ask because your normal teenage crush is a classic parasocial relationship.

The person you're crushing may be real. They might know you a bit, if they're someone from school or your community. But the person that exists in your head is usually made up. Someone who thinks and does things you'd *like* them to think and do. The real person is usually very different, which is why crushes tend not to last if you actually end up chatting with the person in real life.[74]

YADA, YADA!

YAWN!

But while phones didn't 'invent' parasocial relationships, they *do* give you more access to far more people than ever before.

74. Some scientists argue that teenage crushes are how your brain practises for real-life romantic relationships, without all the stress of the real thing. That's right: your teenage crush is the *less* stressful option.

Although, ironically, while phones have led to more parasocial relationships, it's sort of made them less parasocial. Because there's a more direct link between you. Popular people speak to their followers directly and show you more of their lives. It's more personal than seeing a glossy photoshoot in a magazine.

Technology has basically made everyone more accessible. Have you seen those mega-famous video-game streamers join a random fan's game on Fortnite/Minecraft/Roblox/whatever? Fifty years ago, that would have been like an A-list movie star just wandering into your living room and asking if you fancy a game of Twister.

'THAT DOESN'T SOUND SO BAD. WHAT'S MY PARENTS' PROBLEM WITH IT?'

Basically, influencing you is meant to be your parents' job. At least, as far as they're concerned. Whether it's about respecting and considering others, being honest, working hard or not chewing with your mouth open.

So, if complete strangers (to your parents) are

influencing you, in maybe less-than-helpful ways, your parents obviously won't like that.

Who's to say those influential people won't influence you to do *bad* things?

'IF THEY DID, I JUST WOULDN'T DO IT.'

I don't doubt it. Many parents don't trust their kids enough to know right from wrong. It's probably a bad habit they learned from when you were young enough to try to stick your fingers in plug sockets or drink the stuff from under the kitchen sink.

The problem is, to say:

NO, I WON'T DO THAT BAD THING,

you have to *know* someone is influencing you to do it.

Unfortunately, we often don't. And, frequently, neither do those doing the influencing.

'WAIT – WHAT?'

Yeah, it's confusing. Let me explain.

Say you were thinking of getting an expensive pair of trainers but weren't 100 per cent sure.

Then you see someone you really like (your favourite singer, athlete, YouTuber) wearing those exact trainers. Would that make you want to buy them more?

'PROBABLY.'

Precisely. The trainers haven't changed in any way, but you now want to buy them, because someone you admire also likes them.

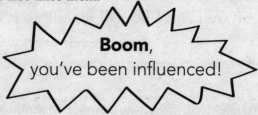

Boom, you've been influenced!

But then: breaking news! Those particular trainers are dodgy. If you wear them too long, they turn your feet purple.

The celeb who endorsed them didn't know this. They didn't make the things. But that doesn't matter. Now you've got less money, useless trainers and purple feet. All because someone influenced you.

So you can be influenced to do things with negative results, even if nobody means that to happen. That's why the influence of others is such a big deal.

'EVERYONE KNOWS INFLUENCERS ARE ALWAYS ADVERTISING AND ENDORSING STUFF, THOUGH. THAT'S HOW THEY MAKE MONEY.'

True. Influencers usually use the influence they have to influence their followers to buy things. Whoever sells those things gives them money to do exactly that. That's basically how the whole system works.

But influence isn't something that can be turned on and off whenever is convenient. It's a 24-hour gig.

I mentioned the trainers example, but that was a silly

thing I made up. In the real world, this is can be much more serious.

Basically, many influencers are often beautiful women in beautiful places.[75] And really, who can blame them? We all want to be liked by others, and like it or not, our physical appearance is a big, important part of that. That's *especially* true for young women. Our society puts pressure on women in particular to be as good looking as possible.[76]

That's unhealthy enough already. But now, thanks to phones, young women can spend hours scrolling through Instagram, looking at posts by beautiful influencers, with their amazing lives and all their admirers. Eventually, a young woman's brain might think:

THAT'S WHAT
I SHOULD LOOK LIKE.

But these alluring posts don't show the search for the ideal location, the set-up of the ideal lighting, the buying

75. Again, it's worth emphasizing that many influencers are people with a knack for creating inspired, entertaining or meaningful content that people enjoy and benefit from.
76. Obviously, it *shouldn't*. But that's a whole other issue.

of expensive photography equipment, the hundreds of rejected photos, the make-up, the digital filtering and whatever else is involved.

Basically, the young women looking at these posts don't see how much effort goes into removing all the flaws and imperfections that all humans have, in some form.

You know whose flaws they *do* see? Their own. Which *should* be fine.[77] But instead they seem *much* worse than they are when compared to these beautiful influencers.

And many young women are experiencing mental health problems, like serious body image issues, as a result. As in, they become extremely unhappy with their bodies because they want – *expect* – them to look like how all those influencers' bodies look.

Basically, being unhappy that your own body isn't as impressive as an influencer's is like being upset because your pet dog isn't a dragon. I mean, of *course* it's not a dragon! It'll never be a dragon. They *don't exist*!

---

77. In an ideal world, being ashamed of your physical imperfections should be like being ashamed of having two nostrils.

But it's hard to tell yourself that when you're constantly bombarded by images of glamorous people online, cheerfully riding dragons through the sky, saying,

YOU DON'T HAVE ONE OF THESE? WOW, WHAT A LOSER!

It's like that, except with your own bodies. Which is, you know, much worse. It's why we use the term *impossible* beauty standards.

It leaves many young women with a sense of inferiority, failure, low status and a seriously warped and negative view of their own physical form, which can have some seriously harmful effects on mental health.

This applies to young men too. There are plenty of buff, muscled influencers providing laughably difficult body goals. But this usually has a different spin, as we'll see later.

'SO PHONES *ARE* BAD FOR MENTAL HEALTH. MY PARENTS ARE RIGHT?'

Well, in a sense. But, again, this isn't a new problem. Air-brushed magazine covers and dangerously thin supermodels have been setting impossible beauty standards for quite some time. There was a lot of dragon riding in the old days too.

But if you've got your phone, impossible beauty standards are only ever a few screen swipes away. And while they've made impossible beauty standards more common, phones have also made impossibly beautiful people much more *relatable*. We can interact with them directly now, via posts and comments and likes. So their influence will be even more potent.

But, as ever, there's another side to the story. Remember, while phone use can harm your mental health, there's also evidence suggesting it can *improve* it.[78] Once again, it depends *how* you use it.

Some young people are *passive* users. They scroll through other people's content, like those posts from the glamorous influencers and . . . nothing else. They

78. See Chapter 1.

don't contribute anything of their own to the 'discussion'. This can cause issues, as we've seen.

If you're an *active* user, if you engage with others and put yourself 'out there', it seems to protect you more from the negative bits.

It comes back to sociability and status. If you're just looking at other people's posts, it's like you're part of a conversation where everyone's talking about the good stuff they've done, while you stay silent. That can make a person feel lonely and low status. *Especially* if all you're looking at is other people being all beautiful.

But if you get involved, saying things like:

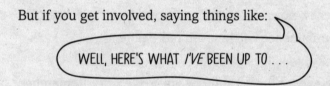

WELL, HERE'S WHAT *I'VE* BEEN UP TO . . .

and people react positively, now you feel accepted and liked. Something we know your brain enjoys. So your mental health is more protected.

Basically, the influence of others isn't so powerful if you feel **you have influence of your own.**

'SO CONSTANTLY BIGGING MYSELF UP WITH MY PHONE IS *GOOD* FOR ME?'

Well, it *can* be. Despite what some parents and grumpy adults think.

After all, everyone who enjoys success and influence, particularly online, must be someone who thought, at some point:

> PEOPLE SHOULD PAY ATTENTION TO ME, BECAUSE I'M GREAT.

And it all spun out from there.

So I guess that's something you *should* be influenced by? Making your online relationships more like traditional ones, where you *contribute* to discussions, not just sit there and get talked at.

We could all do with having *some* influence. And as long as everyone with influence remembers to never misuse or abuse it, it should all be fine.

'ARE YOU JUST TRYING TO SET UP THE NEXT CHAPTER?'

Maybe.

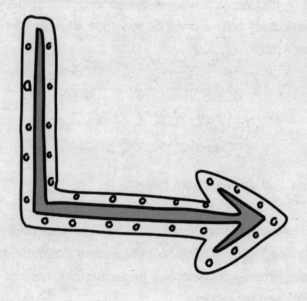

CHAPTER 4

'YOU SHOULDN'T BE LOOKING AT THAT!'

So far in this book I've shared a lot of information with you. **That brings us to another important thing:** using your phone to access information and content that you *shouldn't* be looking at.

According to your parents, at least.

Thanks to your phone, you're able to get to a whole world[79] full of information – more than any other young person in history could ever have hoped for. But while having all that information and material at your fingertips is impressive . . . is it relevant? Honest? Accurate? Is it *safe*?

These are all important questions – ones that many parents (and other adults who make important decisions) worry about constantly. The information and material we see on our phones, especially at your age, can affect how you understand the world, how you think, your beliefs, basically *who you are*. You can't really blame parents for stressing about what sort of stuff you're being exposed to, thanks to your phone.

Are they right to do so, though? Let's find out.

---

79. *Many* worlds if you include the virtual ones. I've read that if *Minecraft* itself were recreated in reality, it would be the size of Neptune.

'I DON'T THINK THAT'S TRUE.'

Need to know how cheese is made? The exact distance between your house and Olympus Mons, the tallest mountain on Mars? You can now find answers to these questions, and tons more bits of obscure and strange information, in mere seconds. While on the bus, while holding a sausage roll. All thanks to your phone.

Sounds great, right? Well, it can be. But it can also be bad.

'WHY? WHAT'S WRONG WITH HAVING EASY ACCESS TO ALL THE INFORMATION IN THE WORLD?'

Well, it would be fine if all that information was correct or useful. Unfortunately, it isn't. Much of the information you see online is absolute guff!

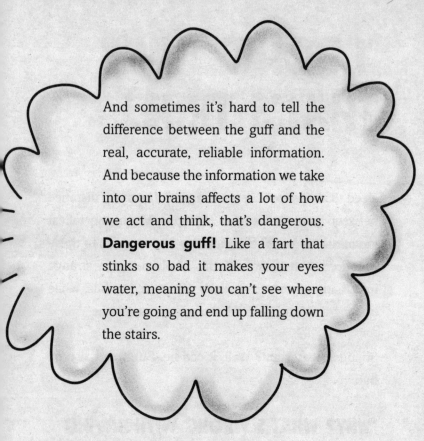

And sometimes it's hard to tell the difference between the guff and the real, accurate, reliable information. And because the information we take into our brains affects a lot of how we act and think, that's dangerous. **Dangerous guff!** Like a fart that stinks so bad it makes your eyes water, meaning you can't see where you're going and end up falling down the stairs.

And many parents worry about this happening to you, thanks to your phone.

To clarify, I mean that metaphorically. I don't mean your parents are worried about you literally falling down the stairs because of a fart. And if they are, they should blame whoever does the cooking in your house, not your phone.

'THANKS, THAT'S A LOVELY IMAGE. BUT WHY WOULD ANYONE PUT WRONG INFORMATION ONLINE?'

That's a very big question, with many different answers. Here are just a few.

A lot of the time, people online are just sharing their thoughts and feelings or their opinions. If someone says:

> I THINK TAYLOR SWIFT IS A GIRAFFE IN DISGUISE,

they're not lying. They're *wrong* – very wrong.[80] But they may genuinely *think* that. So, from their point of view, what they said is true.

Same as if someone says, 'I like . . .' or 'I love . . .' something. There's no way to argue that, as it's just them saying what they feel.

Sometimes information is only wrong because it's old and outdated. Especially with scientific stuff. People

80. As far as I know.

often share information that's believed to be correct *at the time*, but later research proves otherwise.[81]

Ideally, someone would remove all the incorrect information still online. But there's so much of it and it's so mixed up with the valid stuff that it would be practically impossible. It would be like trying to pick all the molecules of fart out of the air so you don't fall down the stairs. So wrong information, much like a powerful fart, just hangs around online, stinking up the place.

This leads to people sharing wrong information *without realizing they're doing so*. They may not know it's wrong or they may be using a source that's unreliable. But they don't *know* that, so they don't question it.

Then there are times when the information being shared is right, but incomplete. Which can make a big difference.

For instance, 'Verity Booglesnap got the highest marks on the class chemistry test'. That could be 100 per cent correct information. Good for Verity! She's clearly very clever.

81. For example, Pluto was reclassified from being a planet to being a dwarf planet in 2006, but you still regularly see it referred to as a planet.

But, ah, this information is incomplete! It should say 'Verity Booglesnap got the highest marks on the class chemistry test *because she stole answer sheets*'. Turns out, Verity is not clever; she's a massive cheat!

Two technically correct statements, with two *very* different meanings.

Of course, a lot of the inaccurate information online comes from people just making stuff up.

'SO PEOPLE JUST *LIE*?'

Yeah. For lots of reasons.

Maybe you want people to like you but haven't done anything that's worth celebrating? Well, just lie and say you did something amazing.

Are you struggling to convince people to agree with you about something you think is important? Lie about why they should agree with you until they do.

Perhaps you're running in an election and want to turn people against your opponent, who hasn't done anything particularly bad. Just accuse them of some awful stuff anyway and hope people believe it.

This is just the tip of the iceberg. It's definitely not rare, sadly. And every time you go online looking for useful information, this stuff is always lurking.

'HOW DO PEOPLE GET AWAY WITH THIS?'

Well, it's the internet. With phones, messaging apps, group chats, social media and all that, it means anyone, anywhere, can put anything out into the (virtual) world, even if it's utter nonsense. And what can anyone *do* about it?

There are things in place to try to prevent it. Some sites and apps can fact-check, and there are rules and laws against spreading harmful lies about people in public, both in the real world and online. But they can only do so much to stop the constant flood of incorrect information. They're often not much better than a sign saying 'Keep off the grass' next to a popular picnic spot.

It's an ongoing worry for parents and adults everywhere, but it does also seem to be just an unavoidable part of modern life.

However, there's another reason people can get away with spewing inaccuracies and misinformation online . . .

People often **prefer** lies to the actual truth.

'WHY WOULD ANYONE *PREFER* LIES TO THE TRUTH?'

Well, before we get all high and mighty about people being untruthful, you've always been 100 per cent honest with your parents. About everything, ever? Right?

Don't worry, you'd be a bizarre person indeed if you only ever told your parents the complete truth. At your age, you're constantly feeling the urge to be independent, to have control over your own life and situation.

So it's pretty much impossible to not want to keep some things to yourself, to not want to hold on to your own secrets. And if doing this involves a bit of light deception when it comes to your parents? Well, so be it.

And I assure you, your parents do the same. Whether it's:

OH, THAT'S A BRILLIANT DRAWING!

or

IF YOU STARE AT THAT SCREEN TOO LONG YOU'LL GET SQUARE EYES,

or

I'M USING MY PHONE FOR WORK!

Much of the time, it's just easier for parents to lie than explain the complicated truth to their children.

'BUT SURELY THAT'S DIFFERENT TO MAKING UP BIG LIES AND SHARING IT WITH EVERYONE ONLINE?'

Good point. Little 'white' lies that make life easier are completely different to making up untruths and rumours and spreading them far and wide. So why would people *like* that?

It's mostly thanks to how our brains process information and learn things.

While there's no known upper limit on how much knowledge your brain can store, thanks to how it's made, it takes in information slowly, gradually.[82]

That's why you have to keep going to school or have weekly classes that progress through a subject bit by bit. It would be great if we could just look at something once and then remember it forever. You'd only need to go to school for about a week! Turn up, read some

---

82. As impressive as it is, your brain is still a physical object. So, logically, there is only so much space for new connections in a human brain, which means there logically *must* be a limit on how much information it can possibly store. However, nobody's lived long enough to get to it yet.

books, absorb the knowledge. Boom! Job done. See you next year, teachers!

Sadly, we can't do that.

It helps to think of the information we learn as being like food, but for your brain and mind. Food is important: we need it to live. The average human gets through about *half a ton* of food in the space of a year.

But if your parents called you into the kitchen and said:

> WE'VE COOKED YOU HALF A TON OF FOOD, ENOUGH FOR A WHOLE YEAR. EAT IT NOW, BEFORE IT GETS COLD.

. . . would you do it?

'NO! THAT WOULD BE IMPOSSIBLE.'

Exactly. You've only got one mouth, one digestive system, one body. There's *physically no way* to eat half a ton of food in one sitting without killing yourself.

Same applies to your brain and knowledge. If you tried to cram a year's worth of learning into your brain in one go, it would probably melt within minutes and dribble out of your ears, like gruesome grey porridge.[83]

'URGH! THAT'S AN IMAGE THAT WOULD PUT ANYONE OFF THEIR FOOD!'

I know, right?

But that's another good point. Some food is just nicer than other food, right? Things like pizza, chips, cake, ice cream . . . that stuff – it's delicious! So we want to eat *more* of it and often you consume more than you need. Which isn't great. Because in large quantities, such food is bad for you. For your body and health.

And there's the other kind of food, the kind that is *good* for you, for your health. But that you often have to choke down because it's not exactly enjoyable to eat. Stuff like sprouts, kale, bran cereals or porridge (not the grey brain kind).

83. Again, I mean this metaphorically. This won't *actually* happen to your brain. Although what could happen wouldn't be anything good.

It's the same with information and knowledge. Some information we *want* to take in and some we *don't*. And it's much easier to learn the first kind. That's why we have favourite subjects and lessons in school that we tend to do much better at than our *least* favourite subjects.

'WHY DO WE PREFER SOME TYPES OF INFORMATION MORE THAN OTHERS?'

Lots of reasons. **But it sort of boils down to this:** for the millions of years during which our brains were evolving and growing, they weren't using *thinking* to figure out what information from the world was worth keeping hold of.

So what *were* they using? The answer is something mentioned in Chapter 2: *emotion*. The emotion parts of our brain have been around a lot longer than the thinking ones. And they're still very much 'there'.

Which means the thinking and emotion parts of our brain **both contribute to how we deal with information**.

Imagine you're walking home alone through a park and you hear a twig snap nearby. The thinking part of your brain says, 'Hmm, unexpected noise. Based on everything I know about this place, it was probably an animal, like a fox. Nothing to worry about, I'll just keep on going.'

But the *emotional* parts of your brain, they hear the unexpected noise and say:

This has kept our species alive for millions of years. Our ancient ancestors living in the harsh reality of nature didn't know what something was or how it worked; they just needed to know how to react to it.

So, for the longest time, the things we experienced that were *important* were the ones that triggered an emotional response.

Our brains learned that information that triggered an emotional response was **worth saving – worth *remembering*.**

And information that didn't trigger any emotion? Like your 423rd walk to school or what you had for breakfast three weeks ago? It wasn't important. So ignore it.

Even though we *can* think these days, our brains *still* tend to use emotion to work out what knowledge is worth absorbing.

That's why you can't remember anything from an hours-long history lesson about farming methods in seventeenth-century Europe, even if it just finished. But you'll forever remember your first kiss or the time your trousers or skirt fell down in front of the whole school.

'I GUESS THAT MAKES SENSE. BUT WHY DOES IT MAKE PEOPLE PREFER LIES?'

Well, the unfortunate thing is, all that important, useful stuff about the world that we should know? It often doesn't have any *emotional* impact.

Maths is a classic example. You absolutely need maths. But unless you're *really* into it, maths doesn't really trigger any emotional response in your brain. It's basically just numbers moving around, which doesn't make you sad or angry or happy. The emotional parts of your brain basically go

SO WHAT? DOESN'T AFFECT ME, I DON'T CARE.

This makes information about maths hard to remember and absorb. So you have to repeat it and revise it, again and again, so your brain says to itself:

THIS *IS* IMPORTANT! JUST KEEP IT STORED, WILL YOU?

Same with stuff like finance, climate and environment and so on. Your brain has to work harder to absorb and keep information about these things.

Solid facts and truths are like raw vegetables. They're good for us, we'd suffer if we didn't have them,[84] but that doesn't mean we *enjoy* eating them.

The truth is often tricky, complicated or just unpleasant from an emotional perspective. For instance, I'm trying to explain the truth about how the brain does things right now. But just because it's true, that clearly doesn't make it simple.

Similarly, someone you care about could ask if you like their new hairstyle, which they're clearly very happy about. And you tell them you think their hair looks like a porcupine that's been trapped in a washing machine. That may be the truth, but it's not *nice*. That's why we say things like 'the *cold, hard* truth' or '*brutal* honesty' when we know people won't enjoy hearing something, despite it being true.

84. Because, for example, we often have to make big, important decisions about such matters, and if our information about them is wrong, then our decisions will be wrong and have seriously bad results.

But if you're making stuff up? Well, you can make it as pleasing for the emotions as you like. You tell your friend their new hair looks nice, even if it doesn't. What's stopping you? It's all coming from your own mind; there are no rules.

For example, you find a bunch of people worried about climate change. So you say to them:

HEY, GUYS, DON'T WORRY.
IT'S ALL MADE UP!

No doubt they'll be *very* happy to hear that.

From all the evidence we have about climate change, we know this is extremely wrong. But the people you're saying it to will want to believe it anyway. Because *emotions* have now got involved.

And emotions often **overrule the truth.**

Back to the food metaphor. If hard facts are like raw vegetables, then pleasing lies are like junk food. Dripping with saturated fats or refined sugars, it tastes amazing! But . . . well, there are a lot of words to describe junk food, but 'healthy' wouldn't be one of them. Remember, eat too much for too long and it can be *really* bad for you.

And as I said earlier, the same applies if you consume incorrect information for too long. It'll do you lasting damage if you believe climate change isn't real or that vital medicine is all a scam (which many do). You'll end up doing things and making decisions that will genuinely hurt you, and others, in the end.

'SO HOW DO WE WORK OUT WHAT IS MISINFORMATION AND WHAT IS ACTUAL INFORMATION?'

The climate change thing is just one example (although an extremely important one) of misinformation being preferred to the important truths.

In fairness, this sort of thing – people preferring reassuring lies over unsettling facts – has always been an issue with us humans. For example, in the United Kingdom, my home country, it was widely believed that when the British Empire went claiming and occupying other countries in the 1800s, those we conquered actually liked and appreciated us, so we were doing a *good* thing. Many in the UK still insist this was true, despite all the statues and national holidays those other countries now have in honour of whoever managed to eventually kick us out.

Phones have changed the game, though. Now information can be shared with anyone, anywhere on the planet, in seconds. Even if that information is wrong. *Especially* if that information is wrong.

Have you ever heard the phrase

A LIE CAN BE HALFWAY AROUND THE WORLD BEFORE THE TRUTH HAS EVEN GOT ITS BOOTS ON?

It means that lies and untruths can spread much faster than the actual truth, for all the reasons we've discussed. It's certainly valid, but if anything, it's out of date. Now it should be

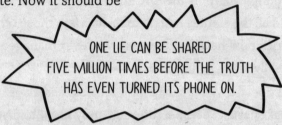

ONE LIE CAN BE SHARED FIVE MILLION TIMES BEFORE THE TRUTH HAS EVEN TURNED ITS PHONE ON.

Like I say, it's an ongoing issue, one your parents are right to be concerned about. But then, it's another thing that also affects your parents. Adults are just as likely to believe misinformation loaded with emotion (as we'll soon see).

If there's one tip to avoiding misinformation online, it's this:

Ask yourself,

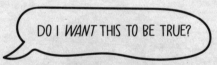

DO I *WANT* THIS TO BE TRUE?

Say you study hard for a test and get the second-highest mark behind another student called, let's say, Jimmy. So you ask your teachers to explain how this happened. And they all say Jimmy must have worked even harder, studied more or understood the subject better, all of which you can do too, if you keep working at it.

But then a friend of a friend says they heard a rumour that Jimmy cheated on the test. To which you say, 'Aha! Now it all makes sense.'

Only it doesn't. What your well-informed teachers said, *that* makes sense. The person you barely know told you a rumour that could easily be utter nonsense. But it's the one you accept as fact. Because it means you *are* the best and you *don't* have to work harder. While the actual truth is that you aren't and you do.

And that's the power of misinformation and how it takes hold.

Basically, if information makes you say:

then take a second. Dig deeper. Ask yourself *why* you want it to be true.

If you can't think of a good answer beyond 'Just because!', then it probably *is* too good to be true.

THAT SOUNDS HARD!

Of course it's hard! That's why hardly anyone does it and lies and misinformation spread so easily.

'OK. BUT . . . ANY OTHER ADVICE?'

Yes, in fact.

Consider the source.

Actually, this is important enough to need its own section.

'ARE YOU SURE YOU CAN TRUST THEM?'

So there's loads of 'untrustworthy' information online, just waiting for you to stumble across it while you look something up on your phone. Like reaching into a packet of crisps and finding a dead moth.

Of course if *that* kept happening, you'd buy your crisps from a different shop. Online information works the same way: if we find that a particular site or platform is spouting nonsense, we avoid it and instead get our information from *trustworthy* sources.

What do we mean by trustworthy, though? It usually means someone or something that can be relied upon. Sometimes that means relying on them to *do* something, like how you *trust* your favourite footballer to score at the right moment. But in this case, trustworthy means we rely on them to be honest and trustful. So, when they tell us things, we *trust* that they're telling us the truth.

However, how do you know someone is 'trustworthy'? It depends on who you ask. And it's a question that's become *especially* important since phones and the internet came along. It's another reason parents worry about what you're looking up with your phones.

If you end up trusting something, or some**one** you shouldn't, **that can be *very* dangerous**.

'SO WHERE *SHOULD* WE GET OUR INFORMATION FROM?'

Well, ask most people where they get their information from online and they'd probably say, 'Google'. But . . . Google is a *search engine*. It *finds* information; it's not the *source*. Thinking you get your information from Google is like thinking the postman is sending you all your birthday cards.

A single Google search can give *millions* of results. How do you know what's trustworthy and what's drivel?

'WELL . . . YOU CAN JUST TELL?'

Often, yes.

Reliable sites and sources are normally used a lot, are popular and have many people working on them (e.g. Wikipedia). They usually look very 'slick' and professional, and are often created by well-known experts working for big 'official' organizations, likc governments and international businesses (e.g. the UK's NHS website).

On the other side, we have things like spam and clickbait[85] lurking at the bottom of actual pages and articles, with titles like '9 amazing facts about grass: number 6 WILL SHOCK YOU!' Not something you'd usually trust to be useful.

---

85. Basically, junk emails and websites, full of obvious nonsense, typically created by cheap software, to entice gullible users into eventually handing over their bank details.

So yes, there are usually obvious differences between trustworthy and untrustworthy information sources.

Unfortunately, phones have confused matters.

'HOW DO PHONES MAKE THINGS MORE CONFUSING?'

By making the differences much less clear.

Remember, before phones people usually got their information from print media, like books, magazines, journals and newspapers. Or broadcast media: TV and radio news, documentaries and so on.

Making a book, TV show or newspaper and putting it out into the world requires a lot of time, effort and resources, from *many* people. There are also laws and regulations about what they can and can't say or share.

Of course you *can* spread bad information via TV shows. It happens often. But doing so takes considerable work, money and effort. And there are consequences for doing so (if you get caught), like hefty fines.

Also, a well-made TV news programme used to look *very* different to what you got when ordinary people made their own shows.[86] Same with professional magazines versus homemade pamphlets.

As a result, people thought print media and broadcast media were more valid and reliable than anything 'amateur'. Most adults still think this today.

Phones have thrown this out of whack, though. These days, everyone has access to the latest tech and apps, which can make anything look 'slick' and professional. Graphically impressive credits? Well-balanced lighting? All are just a button-push away.

So now, when you see a polished video explaining important things in your feed, it could be the work of a well-known news platform, like the BBC or CNN, *or* a ranting maniac with a decent phone camera and some OK design skills.

It's harder than ever to tell. And if it all looks the same, how's anyone meant to know what to trust?

---

86. Look up 'public access TV' from America to see exactly what I'm talking about.

'WELL, WHY WOULD ANYONE TRUST A SINGLE PERSON OVER A BIG OFFICIAL NEWS ORGANIZATION?'

Good question!

We know our brains want connections, interactions, status and emotional responses, right? Well, as a result, we usually prefer information that comes direct from *other people*. If another person, especially one we care about or respect, shares information about something (or *anything*), we're more willing to accept it than if it came from literally anywhere else.

After all, our brains are more likely to absorb information that causes us to react emotionally. And we find other people *emotionally engaging*. As we've seen, we tend to prioritize, focus on and remember things that make us experience feelings, that 'engage our emotions'. And other people are great for this. Our brains are good at detecting (and sharing) the emotions of others, thanks to facial expressions, body language, tone of voice and so on.

That's why you have classes with teachers rather than just a list of books and websites to look at. That's why

TV news and weather reports still have humans, not words on a screen.

So why would anyone trust a single person over a big news organization? *Because* they're a person. One we can relate to. That's how our brains work.

'BUT DON'T OUR PHONES MAKE US INTERACT WITH PEOPLE *LESS*?'

Not quite. I said phones usually mean less *face-to-face* communicating. But online communication still definitely affects us, because that human connection is still there. In fact, thanks to phone cameras, video/streaming sites, and apps like TikTok and FaceTime, online communication is closer to 'real' face-to-face communication than ever. We *can now* see people's face and body, and hear their voice online, which means more emotional information is communicated. So it affects us even more.

In fact, you're a young person, right? I'll bet you get a lot of your information from specific people online, like YouTubers, TikTokers, influencers . . . people like that.

'WELL, I—'

You need to say 'yes' here or the next bit doesn't work.

'FINE! YES, I GET MY INFORMATION FROM PEOPLE LIKE STREAMERS.'

I knew it!

'BUT WHY'S THAT BAD? IF WE'RE LISTENING TO SPECIFIC PEOPLE, WE'LL ABSORB INFORMATION BETTER. THAT'S GOOD, ISN'T IT?'

Yes, in a sense. *Assuming* what they're saying is correct.

That's really important, because, as I keep saying, the information we absorb directly affects our thinking, our beliefs, our understanding. Basically, who we are! After all, think of how many people you know whose whole look and style is based on a TV or music star they just took a liking to.

So how do we *know* the information these individuals share with the world is correct and *safe*? The answer is . . . we don't, usually.

Remember, the big news and information sites certainly aren't perfect, but they still have many people checking and double-checking any information they end up sharing, so they can be as confident as possible that it's correct. At least in theory.[87]

An individual person doesn't have any of that. Anything they want to tell other people, regardless of how ludicrous it may be, they can record on their phone, put online and . . . that's it.[88]

Basically, information from a single person can be *much* less reliable.

---

[87]. Although you can get around this by being sneaky. Like, instead of saying, 'Verity Booglesnap smells like rancid milk,' they can say, 'Verity Booglesnap has been accused of smelling like rancid milk.' The second one is harder to argue. Poor Verity!

[88]. Online platforms have rules and restrictions about what can be shared, but they're often tricky to enforce and have numerous workarounds. So they're not *that* effective.

'PEOPLE DON'T JUST FLAT-OUT LIE, THOUGH, DO THEY?'

Don't they? Because many do. Constantly.

You've probably encountered at least one in real life. Maybe they're a friend of yours?

You know how it is: Monday morning in school, you're chatting with friends about whatever happened over the weekend. But, uh-oh, here comes Jimmy. Jimmy Gibberish. He tells you how he found a £10 million Pokémon card in a bin, so he bought a mansion. Which suddenly burned down. So he had to move back to his old house.

A busy weekend for a 13-year-old.

Certain people have always talked endless nonsense. Why? Presumably they want attention – and happily tell outrageous whoppers to get it. But now these people exist in a world of phones.

In a way, that's bad for them. Now everyone can easily *check* their outrageous claims. A 13-year-old who bought a mansion would surely have made the news. And you can't pretend that your fit boyfriend or girlfriend 'goes to a different school' when they should be easily contactable on Snapchat.

On the other hand, when you can use things like Photoshop, and everyone interacts via screens, it's much *easier* to convince people to take your nonsense seriously. You can take up online pranking or trashposting,[89] or go darker and become a troll.

---

89. It's not usually called *trash*posting but something I'm not allowed to say.

'BUT EVERYONE KNOWS THESE PEOPLE JUST MAKE STUFF UP. NOBODY TAKES THEM SERIOUSLY.'

Oh, you'd be surprised!

But let's say you're right. Even if hardly anybody takes such bunkum-peddlers seriously, *they're* not really who we should worry about. It's the people who *do* take it seriously we need to be wary of. Even if they often speak the truth. Or what enough people *believe* is the truth.

'HANG ON, I'M CONFUSED!'

Yeah, it's baffling. So let's use an example. We've already seen how young women are harmed by online influencers, right? Let's look at men.

Young men are constantly told that they need to be 'masculine' or 'manly'. Which usually means being strong, tough, powerful, good at fighting, never crying or showing feelings, having cool cars and so on. 'Real men' are, or do, all this.

The thing is, when we look at the science, it's nonsense. A guy with long blue hair, nail varnish and a model train collection is as much a 'real man' as some beefy wrestler with a neck like a tree trunk. But, for various daft reasons, the world keeps insisting that only the *second* guy is a 'real man'. So young men feel constantly pressured to be like that.

Forcing yourself to be something you aren't? Holding in all the emotions you feel? All because countless adults (and yes, many parents) insist you *should*? The constant effort and stress of this can be *brutal* for your mental health.

'OK. BUT . . . WHAT'S THAT GOT TO DO WITH SHARING INFORMATION?'

Well, 'all men should be a certain way' is a good example of wrong, harmful information that keeps getting shared anyway.[90] Phones have only made it worse.

---

90. Also, men are human beings; they have countless different qualities and traits that all add up to make one unique individual.

To be more specific, let's imagine a male influencer, whose output is all about how he's a 'real man'.

'Manliness' is often displayed by big muscles, fighting skills, a car collection – stuff like that. Even though none of that is anything to do with being a man, many insist otherwise. To emphasize the ridiculousness of this, imagine an influencer who shows he's a 'real man' by, let's say, punching sharks.

Sounds daft, right? But I bet that's not even a top ten 'most ridiculous thing you've seen online'.

So, this influencer – let's call him 'Shark Bait' – constantly posts videos of himself punching sharks to show how much of a man he is. He also shares advice and information about how to punch sharks yourself – like swimming technique, building upper body strength and facing your fears – which, in fairness, may be genuinely useful.

However, evidence reveals many young men feel constantly stressed and anxious because the world has convinced them that being anything less than a 'real man' means they're a huge failure. So they see this influencer and think, 'This guy punches sharks! He's definitely a "real man". So, I should be punching sharks. And he's telling me how to do it. I should subscribe to his channel!'

And they do. Because he's telling young men what they want to hear. But remember, if you hear something you want to hear, it's more believable and more memorable than something accurate but uncomfortable.

And so this 'Shark Bait' influencer acquires a very big following. Which, thanks to our super-social brains, gets other young men thinking, 'This guy has so many followers! He must be on to something.' But this often means they trust him even if he isn't being truthful. Even if he starts being genuinely harmful.

How might this happen? I mean, he's already telling people to punch sharks. Well, some people say that another way to be a 'real man' is to be desired by as many women as possible.

However, in reality, most women don't feel that punching sharks is cool or impressive. So they certainly wouldn't approve of someone doing it all the time. The shark-punching influencer, therefore, has a problem. His whole 'real man' status depends on women desiring him for his shark-punching skills . . . but they don't. And aren't shy about saying so.

To resolve this dilemma, he might start insisting, publicly, via his online output, that all women are actually idiots, who should be treated like objects. Why? Well, if that's true, it means what they say about not desiring him can be ignored. Because, according to this influencer, women are just too simple to know what they like, or don't like.

Let's be clear, this is wrong. On every level. So is anyone who says it, even if they are a prominent influencer. But the thing is . . . who's going to stop him? He's in full control of the stuff he puts online. All he needs is his phone.

One guy doing that is bad enough. But he has millions of followers who respect and admire him, meaning they can end up agreeing with his anti-women views. Basically, you get countless young men believing something genuinely dangerous, because one person convinced them it was right. That he was right.

Human history has countless examples of women suffering horribly, thanks to men who believed they weren't important enough to matter. So, hopefully you can now see why one person having that much 'influence' can end up being very harmful indeed.

'SO WE'LL BELIEVE WRONG, HARMFUL THINGS . . . JUST BECAUSE OF WHO SAYS THEM?'

Absolutely. Especially if it's people we admire. And because phones give us much more control over how others 'see' us, it's much easier for people to *be* admired. We can choose to only ever show our good qualities and exclude the bad.

Similarly, phones make it easier to find people who say what we want to hear. We find a few individuals who regularly say things that we like, that make us feel good, watch a few of their vids, then the TikTok or YouTube algorithms do the rest: fill your feeds with similar folk, all of whom say things we want to hear.

So we end up liking, admiring and eventually trusting a lot of people who say and do things we like, that we have strong emotional reactions to.

But while we may have good reasons for liking or admiring someone . . . that doesn't mean they're definitely *trustworthy*. Emotional connections don't work like that, as we've seen.

Our brains prefer the stuff that's comforting, reassuring. That stuff is emotionally rewarding. Unfortunately, it's also often **wrong.**

'SO WE CAN'T TRUST INFORMATION WE GET FROM A SINGLE PERSON?'

Oh no, you definitely can. Everyone has useful information and experiences, which they can share; and if they share it in an engaging way that gets you listening, even better. But nobody can tell you useful stuff about *everything*. And it's always worrying if they say they can.

Also, one person being correct about *everything*? Our brains just can't do that. So much of their stuff will be just opinions, based on their own experiences and personal beliefs. Which often means they're hilariously wrong about a lot of things. But if we trust this person enough, we still accept it all.

Take me, for example. I wrote this book to share my information with you. But this book, while technically about phones, focuses mostly on brains. And you can hopefully trust me to tell you about brains. I've been studying and talking about them for *decades*!

However, if this book was instead about playing cricket, nuclear reactors or herding llamas, you should hurl it in the bin! Because I have *no clue* about such things.

But the thing is, there's *nothing stopping me* or anyone else from recording an hour-long video on my phone called 'How to herd llamas while playing cricket in a nuclear reactor' and putting it online.

Believing and trusting someone we're emotionally connected to, even when they're wrong, is nothing new. It's how our brains work. But phones have made it more common. Which is, you know, not ideal.

Earlier, I said encountering misinformation online is like finding dead moths in your crisps. This is *worse*. It's like finding dead moths in a bag of your favourite crisps and *eating them anyway*. While telling yourself, 'No, I *like* these new crisps,' as you choke down wings and antenna.

Point is, it's OK to trust certain people to tell you things, but don't rely on them for *all* your information.

Try not to accept everything someone says as a definite fact, regardless of how many people click 'like' on it.

'MY PARENTS INSIST THEY KNOW EVERYTHING AND THINK I SHOULD TRUST EVERYTHING THEY SAY. ARE YOU SAYING I CAN IGNORE THEM?'

Yeah, about that . . .

'YOU'RE TOO YOUNG TO BE LOOKING AT THAT!'

You know what? I've said so much about how the harmful stuff you find online can be hard to spot that I forgot to point out that there are plenty of times when it's really easy. Because *it tells you*!

A lot of stuff online is intended for older people, usually aged 18 or over.[91] Because it's *harmful* to younger people, like yourself. Your youthful brains, unlike those of adults like your parents, are still developing and maturing. Exposing a younger brain to adult content is like trying to use your phone while it's still updating; it's not finished sorting itself out yet, and you shouldn't interrupt the process with stuff it's not ready to handle yet or you'll mess the whole process up.

---

91. Which makes them *legally* adults in most places. But many older adults still regard them as 'kids'. It's confusing.

Or so people think, anyway.

As a result, content meant for older sorts is clearly labelled, usually with a big warning box that pops up, telling you very clearly that what you're about to see is for adult eyes only.[92] And if you click the box to proceed, you're confirming *you* are an adult.

However, if you're *not* old enough, you press the back button and return to the nice, safe internet, suitable for someone of your age, with your brain and its operating system that is still being updated.

Obviously, as a responsible, well-behaved young person who uses their phone 100 per cent safely, you've never encountered anything like this, right?

'WELL, I . . .'

It's OK, I'm just messing. Younger people have been sneakily exploring 'Adults Only' stuff since long before phones and the internet. They've been doing it for as long as humans have existed. And if millions of

92. There are usually laws that say it has to be.

infuriated adults yelling and punishing them hasn't put young people off, what's a pop-up box on a screen going to do?

In fact, telling young people they're too young for something is usually a very good way of making them want to experience it even more.

'WHY WOULD BEING TOLD WE'RE TOO YOUNG MAKE US WANT SOMETHING *MORE*?'

Well, it doesn't happen with *everything*. If a teacher said, 'Don't read *those* history textbooks, they're only for university students!', you'd probably just shrug.[93]

But if it's something that seems exciting, then being told

YOU'RE NOT OLD ENOUGH FOR THAT.

can make it even more enticing.

93. Unless you were *really* into history. And some people are.

What's happening in the brain to cause this? It's partly status, like we discussed in the last chapter. When you're young, being the most 'mature' is usually seen as a big achievement. It means you're 'ahead' of your friends. And what's more mature than seeing stuff you're supposedly too young for?

Our brains also crave autonomy, the feeling of being *in control*. Especially when you're young, when you're figuring out how to do stuff on your own. Meanwhile parents, school rules and laws that say you're too young for pretty much anything mean you have as little autonomy as possible. So anything that reduces it further, like being told 'You can't see/do that, you're too young,' means you'll want to see and do it even more.

And then there's basic human curiosity. Young brains *need* to experience new things, and learn more about the world, particularly if it promises to be emotionally rewarding. Because, as we've learned, our brains think emotionally engaging stuff is important. So if something is declared off limits, most young people will want to know 'why?' and try to find out.

'IF ONLINE AGE LIMITS AND RESTRICTIONS MAKE US WANT TO SEE SOMETHING *MORE* . . . WHY DO WE EVEN HAVE THEM?'

Valid question.

For the record, most of the time they *are* there to protect you. Just because they don't *work* doesn't mean nobody wants them to.

Sometimes they're to protect the creators of the content you're not supposed to view.

If someone puts an electric fence around their garden next to a busy street and a child touches it, that's *their* fault. Because how was the child meant to know? But if they also put up multiple signs saying:

DANGER!
ELECTRIC FENCE!
DO NOT TOUCH!

and a child *still* touches it? That's the kid's fault. Or the parents', for not keeping an eye them.

The same can apply to age restrictions and guidelines on online adult material. They might not *stop* young people from accessing it, but those who made it can say, 'Hey, we tried.'

It happens a lot. Look at the *Grand Theft Auto* (*GTA*) video games. They have an 18+ age rating, but if you think their massive success is purely due to adults and older people playing them, I've got a definitely-not-stolen car to sell you. Basically, a lot of people decided to ignore age-related guidelines.[94]

'IF SO MANY PEOPLE JUST IGNORE AGE RESTRICTIONS, WHAT'S THE POINT OF THEM?'

Well, there are still certain things that most agree young people *shouldn't* be exposed to until they reach a certain age.

94. Not that most parents *want* to ignore them. But when the rest of the world is doing so, they can end up thinking, 'What's the point?'

Swearing, for example. Most parents would not want their young children to swear or to hear anyone swearing, and people tend to go along with that. Anything with swearing in it tends to get an automatic age restriction. YouTube has rules where anyone with videos that include profanity (bad language) can risk losing the money they get from adverts. And so on.

Although, *why* is swearing bad? Why do certain words have this strange dark power? Well, that is something people are still trying to work out.[95]

But age restrictions on swearing are also confusing because many parents and adults have very different ideas about when and where, and at what age, swearing is acceptable.

It also doesn't help that parents can't control when other adults swear in public places. In a sense, swearing is like the audio version of screen time: your parents worry about you hearing it, but they also can't do much to *prevent* it. So nobody could blame you if this leaves you a bit confused.

95. Scientific studies suggest that our brains process swear words differently, giving them an emotional impact that has lasting effects on us. Although many believe this happens because parents get angry when they hear swearing, so we learn that they're 'special' words. Which would mean swearing is only bad because *parents make it so*. Try telling them this; see which words they reply with.

Also, if you choose to swear when talking with your friends, who's going to stop you? It used to be that a parent or teacher might overhear you and threaten to wash your mouth out with soap and water.[96] But in the privacy of your own snap and group chats, that's not an issue.

So yeah, the rules around swearing can be a bit baffling.

'IT'S NOT JUST SWEARING THAT LEADS TO AGE RESTRICTIONS, THOUGH.'

True. Another obvious one is violence.

Violence is definitely something that young people should be protected from, right?[97] If young people see too much violence, there's a big risk they'll become violent themselves. That's what many parents believe, anyway. Unfortunately, thanks to your phone, the most brutal, visceral violent content is only ever a few swipes and taps away.

96. Something which, if they'd actually done it, would have been *much* more damaging and traumatizing than swearing.
97. Seeing it, I mean. Young people should *definitely* be protected from experiencing actual violence directly.

Again, though, parents and adults in general give you a *lot* of mixed messages here. It seems like some violence is acceptable, but not others.

Remember earlier, when I talked about the chimps fighting? I was actually describing a scene from a nature documentary. Creatures that look quite like humans literally *beat each other to death on screen*! Then *eat each other*! And intelligent adults saw this and said:

> YES, THIS IS VERY INFORMATIVE. WE SHOULD PROBABLY SHOW THIS IN SCHOOLS.

But if it's a much-less-realistic cartoon showing something similar, countless parents would have a screaming meltdown at the very *idea* that their children may see it. What's the thinking behind such different reactions? I'm sure there is some, but I'm not sure what it is.

Then there's the idea that seeing violence *makes you* violent. Parents have been worried about this for a very long time.

Phones have been attacked for this, obviously, but for a while the go-to target for parents was video games.

This idea that playing violent video games made young people violent themselves was *everywhere* when I was your age. So much so that when a violent crime made the news,[98] some newspaper somewhere would find out that the offender had played violent video games at some point. Then they'd shout that this was clear proof that video games were indeed creating a young generation of violent thugs.

You don't get that so much now, thankfully. Probably because video games are just everywhere. Like phones, they're part of life, not so much a 'scary new thing' any more.

Many parents today were, like myself, video-game-playing young people during the whole 'video games cause violence' phase, so it's harder to stay suspicious of something when you've been a part of it.

The idea that there's a link between violent video games and violent behaviour has been studied a lot – so far, there's no clear evidence to support the idea, let alone confirm it. There's even some evidence to show that the opposite happens and they can be *good* for you.

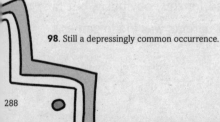

98. Still a depressingly common occurrence.

'VIOLENT CONTENT CAN BE . . . *GOOD* FOR US?'

Not always. But sometimes.

With video games, parents fear that making a fictional character do violent, destructive things in a virtual world will eventually make you want to do the same in the real world. However, evidence shows that, sometimes, the opposite happens. Playing violent video games *reduces* your aggression.

There are a lot of things in modern life that are stressful and frustrating, but that you can do nothing about.[99] So if you can play a video game and obliterate hundreds of alien soldiers or knock seven bells out of a musclebound demon warrior, *that* helps.

It's a safe way for you to express anger and frustration. It provides *catharsis*, which is where strong emotions that you've been holding in, and building up, are released, usually in a safe and healthy manner. It's like sticking a

99. Like dropping a phone and cracking the screen, getting unfairly yelled at by a teacher, missing the bus. And the fact you can't do anything about them makes them *more* frustrating. And this builds up.

pin in a massive painful mental blister in your mind, so the gunk leaks out slowly, providing relief, rather than eventually bursting because of the pressure build-up and . . . making a mess.

Things like contact sports (rugby, boxing, martial arts) provide pretty much the same thing – and have done for centuries. And parents usually encourage you to get stuck into such activities, such *games*. But when it's done in a virtual world, where *literally nobody can get actually hurt*, suddenly it's bad?

'YOU MAKE IT SEEM LIKE AGE RESTRICTIONS ARE BASICALLY POINTLESS?'

Ah, no. I wouldn't go that far.

Just because something is confusing, it doesn't mean it's not necessary. Some people might argue whether a speed limit should be 20 or 30 miles per hour, but they'd both agree that 100 miles per hour is definitely too fast.

Age restrictions are sort of the same.

The line between when something is 'too young' and 'old enough' is often hard to pin down. **But it doesn't mean there *isn't* a line or shouldn't be one.**

Being exposed to certain stuff before you're mature enough can indeed be harmful.

'OK, SO *HOW*, EXACTLY, DOES SEEING STUFF THAT'S TOO "ADULT" FOR US CAUSE HARM?'

The thing to remember is this: your young brain is still developing, still maturing. And this process, like learning and taking in knowledge, is *meant* to be gradual and slow. That's why it takes over a decade until it's 'finished'. While this is happening, your brain has stronger emotional reactions to things, and much less experience at handling them, than an adult brain.

This makes your mental health more vulnerable too. Because too many negative emotions are a big factor in mental health disorders. So is an overtaxed, sleep-deprived brain. So is a brain that's constantly changing.

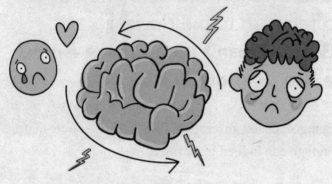

All these things apply at your age.

So while it's tempting, *really* tempting, to want to experience things meant only for adults, such things can hit your developing brain hard. *Too* hard. It's like trying to drive a car when you've never had any lessons. No matter how confident you are, how little fear you have, you're much more likely to get hurt when behind the wheel than someone old enough to have a licence.

While this has been an issue for countless years, at least in the past it was much harder for young people to access age-restricted things because there was someone there, usually another adult, to stop you. If you wanted to do something like drink alcohol or rent a gory movie, you had to somehow convince the adult in the shop you got such things from to give them to you. And that's hard.

But now there's all sorts of adult content online, and thanks to your phone the only thing between you and it is a box saying 'You promise you're old enough, yeah? Just tick that box, then.'

'WITH OUR PHONES, WE'RE JUST LOOKING AT STUFF. SURELY IT'S NOT *THAT* BAD?'

You'd think so, but that's not how it works. We covered this back in Chapter 1. And in this very chapter, where we saw how information can affect you. Because you're still young, your brain's still developing, you're still figuring out your identity. So anything you take in now can have a much bigger and more lasting effect on you.

It's like, imagine if you tried cheese for the first time

ever, at the age you are now. But it's *blue* cheese, the kind that smells like a particularly sweaty gym sock. That stuff is for the hardcore cheese fans. You need to build up to it, to eat gradually stronger and stronger cheeses until you're ready for the powerful stilton.

But if you'd never had cheese before and jumped straight to the sock-smelling kind, you'd immediately think cheese is *awful*. Even though most of it isn't. But it's too late now – that first impression has been made. It'll take a lot of time and effort to unlearn this 'cheese is vile' lesson.

Seeing stuff and information online that you're not ready for is like this. Except swap 'cheese' for 'important life experiences'.

It doesn't even need to be 'bad' information, like with the angry male influencer. It can be very well intended, but *still* harmful. For instance, many young people, particularly those with their own mental health issues, like to hear from influencers who talk about mental health. They can help young people understand their issues and feel less alone. And that's mostly great.

But mental health is also a very *personal* **experience**.

Everyone has their own journey and struggles. And if you get *too* into a mental health influencer, you can end up thinking:

> MY MENTAL HEALTH ISN'T GREAT, AND THIS PERSON KNOWS ALL ABOUT THAT. SO I SHOULD DO WHAT THEY DO.

Thanks to your developing brain and identity, this can lead to strange outcomes, where young people start displaying symptoms for mental or brain-related conditions *they don't actually have*. They've just put too much attention into an influencer who *does* have this issue.

This *can* actually happen. Look up news stories about 'TikTok tics', where many young people started displaying tics and twitches typically caused by Tourette's syndrome. Only they didn't have Tourette's syndrome; they were just big fans of a TikTok influencer who did.

Again, it's like your brain is wet cement, and age restrictions are the signs telling people not to walk on it until it's 'set'.

'BUT . . . INFLUENCERS AND MENTAL HEALTH RESOURCES DON'T *HAVE* AGE RESTRICTIONS.'

Indeed. But . . . maybe they should? Because the current approach with age restrictions could be described as both crude and confusing. It seems to be mostly adults who are saying:

WE THINK THAT'S A BAD OR WRONG THING THAT COULD HARM MY KIDS, SO WE DON'T WANT THEM SEEING IT.

But this approach is applied only to certain things, in certain ways, and not others.[100]

---

100. For example, in the UK you're not allowed to drink alcohol in pubs if you're under 18. Unless it's paid for by the adult supervising you. And you're having a meal. And it's a Wednesday. And you've got a green hat on . . . or *something* like that. I lose track.

A more thoughtful approach could be helpful. But it could be a while before we get one. So, in the meantime, just have a think – a proper think – before you use your phone to dive into matters and content that you may be a bit young for. You'll be old enough eventually; there's no rush, honestly.

'AND IF THERE'S ANYTHING I'M STILL CONFUSED ABOUT, I SHOULD JUST ASK MY PARENTS?'

Ah . . . about that.

When it comes to 'adult' content, there's one particular aspect where asking your parents gets rather tricky . . .

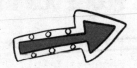

'I'LL TELL YOU WHEN YOU'RE OLDER.'

I'm oddly impressed with myself.

I just wrote several pages about the sort of adult stuff online that you shouldn't be looking at because you're not old enough. And I never mentioned it once.

'NEVER MENTIONED WHA— OH NO! PLEASE DON'T SAY —'

I'm talking about sex! Physical intimacy between two people (at least).

Sex!

'AAAAAARGH!'

Yeah, I know.

Look, *I* don't want to have to talk to you about sex, *you* don't want me to and I'm confident your parents won't want me doing that either.

In fact, many parents *really* don't like anyone talking to younger people about sex. Even when it's supposed to be educational. This means there are many rules and restrictions as to what adults, like me, can and can't say to younger people, like you, about sex.

'THAT SOUNDS LIKE A HASSLE. MAYBE JUST MOVE ON AND TALK ABOUT SOMETHING ELSE?'

That would be easier, sure.

Unfortunately, the issue of young people, like yourself, seeing, sharing and *creating* 'sexual content', with your phones, is a *big* concern for parents, and adults in general. And they've got a point, for once. I can't just skip the whole thing. It's too important.

'WHY IS SEX SO IMPORTANT?'

Well . . . it just is! It's weird.

Because we don't *need* it. It's not like food, drink or sleep: we can go our whole lives without it. But despite this, the typical adult brain spends *a lot* of time thinking about, and figuring out how to get, sex.

But if you're a young person or teenager, that's often when sexual thoughts and urges have the biggest impact on you. Because you *don't really know* what sex is or how it works. Or at least you *shouldn't*. You just know you want it.

'HOW CAN YOU WANT SOMETHING IF YOU DON'T KNOW WHAT IT IS?'

Well, when you hit puberty, your body changes a lot. It's suddenly pumped full of something called *sex hormones*, like testosterone and oestrogen. The hormones flooding your body basically go around flicking switches, powering up all the physical and mental processes that are involved with sex. So you suddenly want to have sex, despite never experiencing it. It's a confusing time.

It's like spending your whole childhood in a remote, beautiful country village from the 1950s, then waking up one morning and realizing you *really* want pizza.

Only it's the 1950s countryside. Where are you meant to find pizza? What even *is* pizza? And you don't want to ask anyone about it because it's strange and embarrassing. So you just put up with it . . . while staring longingly at bread, cheese and tomatoes. You know you want to do *something* with them, you're just not sure what.

Becoming 'sexually aware', thanks to all the puberty-powering hormones in our system, is like this. Only it's not pizza, it's . . . people. You're now physically attracted to others and find yourself – strangely – *wanting* them.

'IF WE DON'T KNOW ABOUT IT, HOW DO WE LEARN ABOUT IT?'

You learn *slowly*. And *carefully*. At least that's how it's *meant* to happen. Sex is so powerful that any experience of it – but *especially* your earliest ones – can have important, lasting effects on you.

Remember the blue cheese example from earlier, and why your first experiences can be so significant? Well, your first encounter with sex is like that, but often *considerably more powerful*!

Your brain is pretty much a blank slate when it comes to sex. At least with cheese you've eaten stuff before. You know how that works. That's not the case with sex, so your earliest encounters with anything sexual will have an even stronger impact. They'll basically be burned into your brain and can affect your whole understanding of sex from then on.

That's why, when it comes to sex, **it's best to tread carefully**.

'IF SEX IS SO IMPORTANT AND EVERYONE WANTS IT, WHY DOES NOBODY LIKE TO TALK ABOUT IT?'

Yeah, that's a tricky one to get your head around. There are many good reasons, but an important one is that sex is something that requires you to be at your most exposed, most vulnerable, most personal. And it's a big deal to discuss these things with anyone. *Especially* with people you already know and might be close to.

Look at it this way: if one day your teacher tried to give a lesson while sat on the toilet with their trousers and pants around their ankles, would you be OK with that?

'NO! THAT WOULD BE AWFUL!'

It definitely would.

Why, though? It's someone you know pretty well. Doing something you know they do. That you do yourself. So what's the issue?

'IT JUST . . . IT'S WRONG!'

I agree with you 100 per cent. As does everybody. Any teacher who tried that would be sacked within minutes and may well end up in jail.

Basically, we humans are very social and love interacting with each other. But we also feel that if it's something so personal and biological, it should be *private*. We all *know* that everyone chews their food and uses the toilet to get rid of what happens to this food when our body is done with it . . . but we don't want to *see* anyone doing any of this or the parts of the body involved. That's why we chew with our mouths closed. And toilets have doors. Which lock.

For most people, sex falls under the umbrella of:

'deeply personal and very biological act that everyone does **but nobody wants to know about anyone actually doing**'.

Which makes talking about it a lot more awkward.

304

This can also be why talking about sex with your parents is such hard work. Remember, when you're a young person, your brain is trying to distance yourself from your parents and their influence as much as it can.

So sex – the most private and personal thing anyone can do – is basically the *last* thing you'll feel comfortable discussing with your parents.

Although if you, and they, *can* overcome your desire not to, discussing sex stuff with your parents (or anyone else you trust) usually *is* a good idea because relying on ideas from your own baffled brain only takes you so far.

That's why people with actual experience who are willing to share their insights with you can be even more useful. As can educational materials, however awkward they may be.

Your brain will keep making you *want* sex,[101] so the more you understand it, the more likely you are to 'get' it. Eventually.

---

101. Although everyone's desire for sex will differ. Some people will even be asexual and not want or need sex at all. You'd think this would make for an easier life, but since most people *do* want sex, asexuals often get flack for being 'weird'. You just can't win.

'BUT I CAN JUST LOOK IT UP ON MY PHONE, CAN'T I?'

You'd think so. After all, you can use your phone to look up pretty much anything – mental health, news and politics, hobbies, fandoms, video games, fashion, study advice – and find helpful information about it online.

But with sex, it's not so straightforward. That's because there's a *lot* of sex-based stuff online. And while some of it will be educational, informative or instructional, a lot of it . . . won't be. It's more for 'entertainment' purposes.

Basically . . . most of the sex content online will be pornography of some sort.

'IS THAT BAD? IT'S ALL THE SAME, ISN'T IT?'

Here's the thing: I can't go into much detail about this in a book aimed at young people without getting into serious trouble.

So, let's talk about wrestling instead.

'WRESTLING?'

Wrestling, like you see in the WWE. On TV and YouTube, starring John Cena, The Undertaker, Roman Reigns, Becky Lynch . . . All that.

You may not like wrestling, but *millions* of people love it. In fact, they are obsessed with it. After all, wrestling involves people with exaggerated, almost ridiculous physiques (like huge, rippling chest muscles), wearing laughably little clothing and getting all oiled up and sweaty. They also say dumb things to each other and act out silly situations.

Then they do very physical things with each other in front of an enthusiastic audience. Things that would do serious harm to a normal person. Sometimes they even use props.

Basically, they turn up in the arena in tight yellow shorts and boots, with a false tan, bellow trash talk at their opponents, then proceed to body slam them to the floor and hit them with a chair.

But it's OK because everyone's a professional performer. It's all planned and there are scripts telling people what to say and do. You just absolutely shouldn't try to do what they do yourself.

Why am I telling you this? Well, replace 'wrestling' with 'pornography' in that first paragraph and *it still makes perfect sense*.

Now imagine you somehow forgot how to interact with your friends. So you watched some wrestling and thought, 'Ah, *that's* how it's done.' So you turn up for school wearing just yellow underpants and wellington boots, with an orange tan, roar some weird threats at your nearest friend, body slam them to the schoolyard floor and beat them across the head with a biology textbook.

They probably wouldn't still be your friend after that.

Basically, learning about sex from pornography is like learning how to talk to your mates from wrestling.

'YEAH, OK. THAT WOULD BE EMBARRASSING.'

Not just embarrassing.

Dangerous!

Unlike food, drink, video games or any other of those things we enjoy, whether or not you have sex always involves someone else's consent. Someone *has* to agree to doing it with us. That's just how it works.[102]

If your only knowledge of sex comes from adult content online, that will *not* give you a very good sense of how it works. It can make you think it's easy or that you're entitled to it so consent isn't important, or that certain behaviours in sex are acceptable when they very much are not. *Particularly* when you're dealing with another young person, like yourself, who doesn't have much, or *any*, experience. You could end up doing stuff that's upsetting.

---

102. Trying to do it with someone without their consent is not so much sex as a full-on crime. We've seen how powerful sex is, *especially* when you're new to it, so someone being made to have sex when they *don't want to*? That can be seriously damaging. Life-changingly so. And if an individual believes them having sex is more important than not ruining someone's life, they're not safe to be around.

'IT SOUNDS LIKE YOU'RE SAYING I SHOULD AVOID SEXUAL CONTENT ENTIRELY.'

Look, even if I *did* think that was a good idea, it would be a pointless thing to say. Young people going through puberty seeking out sexy content is a fact of life. It's always happened. It's just that, thanks to phones, it's much *easier* for you to find and access it now than it ever has been, and parents can do very little about it.

And I'm not saying that if you experience *any* sexual or otherwise adult content it'll ruin you forever. That would be a bit extreme. You'll probably be fine, overall. But that *probably* is important. It means genuine harm is still *possible*.

Basically, as I suggested earlier, it's like young people going through puberty suddenly get a big empty space in their brain, like a folder that needs filling with files labelled 'Sex and how it works'.

It's *meant* to be filled slowly, gradually, with useful information, experiences and healthy (if often very embarrassing) interactions, whether they are fumbling sexual encounters or just awkward conversations. But phones mean the folder can be filled *very* quickly with the stuff you find online. And that gives you a very warped view about 'good' sexual behaviour, which can mean you might cause actual harm to others.

For instance, things like pornography can make you think that taking photos of certain parts of your body and sending them to someone you're attracted to is acceptable and something that will make them desire you. It's not just that, though.

It's also very likely **illegal**.

Remember when I said seeing too much 'adult' material is, to your brain, like driving a car without getting your licence first? Well, when it comes to sex stuff, seeing too much adult material and then acting on it – that's like trying to drive a car, with no licence, in the middle of a 100-car demolition derby!

You don't belong there. You don't know what's going on, but whether it's you or others, *someone* is going to get hurt.

'THIS IS THE SORT OF THING PARENTS WORRY ABOUT, I GUESS.'

Yeah, no doubt.

But let's not let them off the hook too easily. They play their part in this as well. So many parents are so resistant to teaching children *anything* about sex that it leaves them even more uninformed about it than they really should be.

But the sex parts of young people's brains don't just switch off because parents don't want them to think about it. Them constantly saying

DON'T LOOK AT THAT!

or

I'LL EXPLAIN WHEN YOU'RE OLDER.

isn't really helping. It's like something's caught fire in your bedroom and they're dealing with it by closing the door so they don't have to look at it.

It leaves young people having to look elsewhere for information about sex. And you'll easily find it online. Where a lot of what you experience is wildly wrong, and often harmful, as we've seen. But you don't know that. Because nobody's told you otherwise!

'SO WHAT DO YOU SUGGEST?'

Look, you're almost certainly going to end up seeing sex stuff with your phone. That's pretty much unavoidable at this point. And it will be, shall we say, *exciting*. And you'll probably want to see more.

But do try and keep in mind that most of the stuff you see with your phone isn't 'real' sex. Not the sort of thing you're likely to end up experiencing. So try not to learn any lasting lessons from it.

CHAPTER 5

'NO PHONES IN CLASS!'

We've looked at the many things your parents worry about when it comes to your phone. But . . . your parents aren't the *only* adults in your life with concerns about your phone.

There are also **your teachers.**

There's a good chance you've had an argument[103] or a disagreement with a teacher about your phone and what you should or shouldn't do with it.

I mentioned this to a few teacher friends of mine, who shared their thoughts on the subject. And it was *very* eye opening. They even got me into the school to speak to the students.

One thing was clear: school, with teachers, is a very different situation to home, with your parents. Different rules apply.

So how your phone affects your time at school – your lessons and education, and relationships with teachers and other students – needs a chapter to itself. Especially because if your parents get involved with how your phone is used in school, they often make things *worse*.

---

103. Full-on arguing with teachers is a *very* different thing to arguing with parents.

'PUT YOUR PHONE AWAY, IT'S DISTRACTING!'

Your school probably has rules and restrictions about phones. Like 'Phones can only be used during break and lunch times'; or 'Phones must be kept out of reach during lessons'; even 'Phones must be handed in at the start of the day and will be returned at the end.'

Unless . . . they don't. Some schools genuinely don't have rules about phones. You can keep it with you at all times. Then there are other schools that are super strict, banning all phones on school grounds at all times.

Most schools fall somewhere in the middle.

'WHY DO DIFFERENT SCHOOLS HAVE SUCH DIFFERENT RULES ABOUT PHONES?'

Schools aren't all the same in any case. A bit like McDonald's, each school will be slightly different.

Is it a state school? Private school? Religious school? School of fish?

How many students? What are their abilities, backgrounds, cultures?

Where is the school? Which region, what country?

All this and more will affect what sort of rules the school puts in place.

Also, remember that phones are still quite a *new* thing. This means the impact they might have on learning and education over a long period of time is still unknown. Will they ruin your memory or attention span? Will they *improve* those things? Are they affecting you in unhelpful ways we've not even noticed yet? We can't be 100 per cent sure about any of these things yet. This makes it much harder for schools to work out what the 'right' rules are.

So some schools will think, 'No phones at all!', just in case they do cause significant issues. Others will go 'Meh' and just roll with them.

There may be different rules for older and younger students. Or the rules might keep changing and being updated, depending on how everyone reacts to them.

Again, this isn't new. Whenever there's something modern and flashy that all the young people get obsessed about, schools impose rules about them. It happened even when *I* was in school, with things like personal stereos[104] and Tamagotchis.[105]

Of course nothing's ever had as big an impact on school as phones. They can just do so much stuff.

But despite all these differences in rules, there's one thing many teachers will agree on. Your phone can disrupt your learning by being a *distraction*.

---

104. Often called a Walkman, they were the original portable music system, with headphones. They played cassettes, which held about an hour's worth of music. Which seemed a lot back then.
105. A digital pet that would 'die' if you didn't 'feed' it. Just . . . look it up.

'YEAH, MY TEACHERS SAY THAT A LOT.'

I bet. But . . . are they right?

In many ways, yes. There have been studies into this. If you put people in an empty room and make them do a task, they'll tend to give 100 per cent of their attention to it. But if you put a smartphone in there with them, even if it's not doing anything, there'll always be *part* of their attention given to it rather than focusing on the task.

Which means phones *are* distracting, right?

'SO PHONES ARE A DISTRACTION, NO MATTER WHAT?'

Well, it's not *quite* that simple. Many people do see these studies as proof that there's something fundamentally distracting about phones. But another conclusion might be:

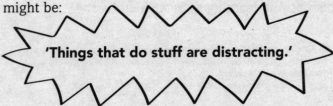

'Things that do stuff are distracting.'

'WHAT?'

Yeah, I could have worded that better.

Basically, a phone isn't a rock or a pot plant. It doesn't just sit there, doing nothing. It *could* do something, at any moment.

Imagine trying to do a task in the same room as a sleeping horse. You *should* be able to give all your attention to the task because the horse isn't doing anything especially distracting right now. But the fact is . . . it *could*. The horse could suddenly wake up and who knows what'll happen then?

As a result, our brain will always give part of our attention to the horse. So it's a distraction. But you wouldn't then say:

> AHA, HORSES ARE
> FUNDAMENTALLY DISTRACTING!

Because . . . that'd be weird.

Basically, having a phone in the same room may distract us from a task (e.g. studying for a test), but it's not a phone thing, it's a *brain* thing.

'I THOUGHT I COULD CHOOSE WHAT I PAY ATTENTION TO. MY TEACHERS KEEP SAYING I CAN.'

Good point. Teachers are always telling students to 'pay attention', which I suppose means they think you can just *decide* to do that. To focus entirely on what they're saying.

And they're partly right. You can choose what to pay attention to. I say 'partly' because you can only do that with *part* of your attention system.

By 'attention system', I mean the part of your brain that decides what you are focusing on, what you're pointing your eyes and ears and 'mind' at. You can only focus on one thing at a time and your attention system is what decides which 'thing' is most important.

But here's the thing:

Your basic brain actually has *two* attention systems.
One of those you control by thinking about it.

The other one, not so much.
**It's controlled by *unconscious*
brain processes.**

These are all the things your brain does without you ever being 'aware' of it. Without even having to think about it.

So we have an unconscious attention system and it takes control over your attention *without* you thinking about it or even realizing it's happening.

Have you ever been in bed at night, alone, and heard an unexpected and unexplained noise? Like a thump from upstairs or a crash from nearby, and you immediately focused on it? Often while also panicking slightly . . .

But did you think to yourself, 'Hmm, that wasn't a sound I usually hear. I'd best pay attention to it in case it happens again'? No, you just *were* paying attention to it. Any thinking about it happened after you were very focused on it.

Your unconscious brain is always doing this. Scanning your surroundings with your senses, looking for anything that *could* be important and giving your attention to it the moment it spots something.

'SO I HAVE *TWO* TYPES OF ATTENTION AND ONE IS MORE POWERFUL THAN THE OTHER?'

It's not so much about power; it's more of a balancing act.

Think of your brain's attention systems as like a human walking a big dog. The human is your conscious attention system, the one you control by thinking about it; it decides where you're going. The dog, your unthinking, subconscious attention system, usually follows along, but it is also always doing its own thing, sniffing around at everything.

And sometimes the dog will sniff or see something it thinks is important, like a squirrel or another dog, and run after it. But the thinking person on the other end of the lead doesn't realize this has happened until it's too late. They've been yanked in a whole different direction and maybe dragged through a bush.

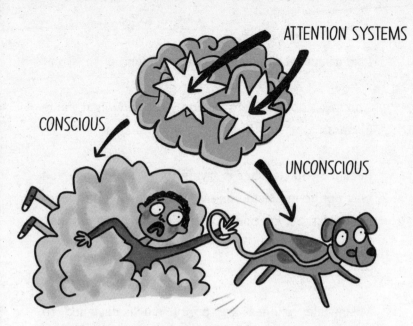

ATTENTION SYSTEMS

CONSCIOUS

UNCONSCIOUS

Your brain's attention system is basically like this: two parts that usually work together, but one has a habit of darting off whenever it notices something important and the other has to pull it back to where it's needed. Staying 'focused' usually involves getting a balance between the two.[106]

What phones do, when they're visible or nearby in class, is they provide the unthinking, 'big dog' part of your attention system with something it really wants to stay focused on (maybe growling at quietly). Because a phone could do something unexpected at any moment.

106. Some people aren't as able to do this. It's like their unthinking attention system is a particularly big and strong dog that's much harder to keep under control. This is why we have attention deficit hyperactivity disorder, ADHD.

Like a squirrel, sitting on a nearby branch.

And this is obviously distracting. *Especially* when you're in class.

Because your teacher is trying to tell you things you may not be interested in, but which you need to learn regardless. So you need to pay *more* attention to them, because your brain will be reluctant to absorb them otherwise.

Meanwhile, phones are pretty much designed to provide fun – stuff our brain actually likes. Stuff that makes the conscious 'dog-walking human' attention system regularly say:

OOH, LOOK AT THAT!

and want to wander over and explore.

That's why, given the choice, most young people will always prefer to know what their phone is saying over what the teacher is saying . . .

Which isn't ideal for when you're trying to learn stuff.

'WHY CAN'T WE PAY ATTENTION TO TWO THINGS AT ONCE?'

Well, paying attention to something – understanding and thinking about it – is a lot of work for your brain. This means we only have so much attention and it can only be directed at one thing at a time.

Many scientists describe this as your attention being a spotlight and your surroundings a large, dark stage where the show is taking place. You're in charge of the spotlight. You can point it at where important stuff is happening or you can jump from place to place and work out what the 'whole stage' looks like.

But it's impossible to light up the whole stage or two parts of it at once. You can maybe keep jumping between two or three things, but even that is pushing it and you'll quickly lose track of what's happening where.

Occasionally, your big dog grabs the spotlight and shoves it towards something unexpected, like someone coughing in the audience.[107]

A-HEM!

So, in a teacher's ideal world, everyone in a class would be directing their attention, their 'spotlight', at them and what's being taught. But what's being taught isn't always something you're interested in hearing, meaning it takes effort to keep your attention on it. And if you're paying attention to something you don't really want to focus on, it's much easier for other, more interesting things to divert your attention away from it.

That's why teachers tend to insist on quiet during lessons. And why they want phones out of sight. Because they're something that you can't help but pay attention to if they're there.

107. If you're wondering why you would take your dog with you when working a spotlight . . . I don't know. That's just how the brain is.

'BUT MY PHONE ACTUALLY *HELPS* ME FOCUS, LIKE WHEN I'M LISTENING TO MUSIC.'

Ah, interesting!

That's another thing many teachers have an issue with: students using their phones to listen to music *during lessons*. Many students insist they *need* to listen to music, as it helps them concentrate.

While everyone learns best in their own way, science suggests that listening to music like this isn't that helpful. Your standard brain can usually only pay proper attention to one bit of sound at a time. So if you've got music playing, with speakers barely an inch from your eardrum, your teacher's voice has little to no chance of getting through to you. So yeah, if you're listening to music through headphones, your teacher can't really do their job.

However, if you're working by yourself, many studies suggest that music (at least chilled, soothing music) can help us concentrate *better* than silence.

Why? Because with this kind of learning, sound and noise aren't involved. And there's no teacher talking to you. So your hearing system just sits there, waiting for something to do. If you're working in silence, it means that any sound that *does* happen stands out a lot more, making it even more distracting. Playing calm, chilled-out music in the background solves this problem. It gives your unthinking attention something harmless to focus on.[108] A bit like giving the big dog a toy to keep it quiet while you get stuff done.

So, yes, if you're using it to listen to some calming music, that's an example of your phone helping you concentrate rather than distracting you. So you could well say your phone is helping you learn.

'BUT THAT'S NOT THE ONLY THING MY PHONE IS GOOD FOR IN SCHOOL AND LESSONS.'

Yeah, phones do a lot of things. That's actually a common argument for why phones should be allowed in school.

108. It'll be different for everyone, but music like pop, metal or hardcore rap often give your brain too much to deal with. Look up 'lo-fi beats', which is what I'm listening to as I write this.

Actually, some people go further and question whether lessons are even necessary.

Why learn maths? Your phone is a calculator that's always in your pocket.

 Why learn geography? Google Maps can show you anywhere on Earth, in seconds.

Why learn other languages? There are apps to translate them all, in real time.

And so on.

Why do we need to learn anything when phones can do it for us? It's tempting to think like this. Particularly when actually learning things feels like a struggle. But the problem with this is . . . why stop there?

Why play any sport? You can watch experts do it on YouTube.

 Why go on holiday? You can see all manner of beautiful places on Instagram.

Why walk anywhere? Just get an Uber.

And so on.

But most people would think if you're letting your phone do all the work, it's nowhere near as good. Playing sport isn't about just finding out who wins and technical skill, it's about exercise and activity, teamwork, competition and lots of other fun stuff. Going on holiday isn't just about seeing different places, it's about experiencing new things, exploring, relaxing and indulging.

By doing it all via your phone, **you lose all the benefits you get from doing it in person.**

Like it or not, the same applies to *learning* stuff. If you don't do it yourself, you don't develop, grow or acquire new skills and abilities. Playing sports, like football, helps you develop fitness, coordination, planning. Travelling in person allows you to better understand other cultures, languages and customs.

And you *could* just use your phone for things like long division or the impacts of seventeenth-century European farming methods. But if you don't put the effort into figuring out these things yourself, you risk losing your ability to figure things out *at all*.

Your brain often learns by doing, and if you don't make it do something . . . it can't do it.

Does that make sense?

It's like, imagine if, instead of eating your food yourself, your parents carried on feeding you until you were 18, with the old

> OPEN WIDE, HERE COMES THE AEROPLANE!

method. That would be much less effort for you. Would you like that?

I'm guessing . . . no. Just because something is easier, that doesn't make it *good for you*. If you did let your parents do this, you'd likely never even work out how to use a knife and fork. And school lunchtimes would be *very* weird.

Relying on your phone to do all your thinking and learning amounts to the same thing.

'OK. BUT SHOULD I BE ALLOWED TO BRING MY PHONE INTO CLASS OR NOT?'

Well, as we've seen, and despite what many teachers say, there are times when it's helpful to have your phone in class. Sometimes *very* helpful!

Many schools have realized this and now incorporate them into teaching. So you get email updates, lesson schedules, ebooks, shared documents, lesson and presentation recordings, virtual classrooms. These are all useful educational resources that you can use with your phone.

But as we've seen (and I'm sure you've experienced), there'll be plenty of times when your phone does disrupt lessons. Because it does much more than just the useful stuff, and it's hard to get to grips with quadratic equations when the group chat is bombarding you with funny memes.

'SO MY PHONE IS BOTH USEFUL *AND* DISRUPTIVE? HOW DOES THAT WORK?'

Look at it this way. A carpenter can't do their job without a hammer, right? So obviously they'd say a hammer is useful. But if they tried to eat their dinner or clean their car with the hammer, it would be the opposite of useful.

And just like how a carpenter must know when and when not to use a hammer, learning when *not* to use your phone – to just put it down and ignore it – is an important skill. And it's one you can probably learn in school, by having it with you in class, but not using it when your teacher says.

Because while they might be annoying, overly strict, even flat-out wrong from time to time, your teachers are still people who know how to teach you things. They've done this before, they've been extensively trained for the job, they know what the lesson involves and what it needs to cover, and what you'll need to know to pass all the inevitable tests and stuff.

So they'll probably know when you should be paying more attention to the lesson and less attention to your phone. That means you should at least listen to them on this matter.

This isn't to say your phone is *never* useful in school, because it clearly can be. But remember, like a hammer, your phone is a tool. A very useful one, but still a tool.

Which means *you* should be in charge of your phone
and be deciding when it should and shouldn't be used.

'WAKE UP! IT'S TIME FOR SCHOOL!'

Do you find yourself struggling to get to school in the morning? Is it hard work, simply lifting your head off the pillow? Do you often just lie there, staring at the ceiling, thinking:

NOT *THIS* AGAIN . . .

Does this sound familiar to you?

'YEAH, IT DOES.'

Unsurprising. Young people like yourself are virtually *guaranteed* to not get enough sleep a lot of the time, which isn't ideal. We mentioned this back in Chapter 1, but it's so important it needs repeating.

Basically, you *need* sleep. It's not an optional extra, like a designer phone case with a cartoon kitten on it.

Sleep is when your body rests and recuperates from the day you've just had, **allowing it to grow, heal and repair.**

Sleep is also when the new memories and experiences you've gathered while awake are sorted out and properly organized in your brain, so they don't float about, causing confusion. Like librarians sorting out a big delivery of new books: they put them on the correct shelves, rather than in a big heap by the main doors.

Basically, when you're asleep a lot happens in your brain and body that's really important for your health, well-being and ability to function normally. Which is why, if you don't get enough sleep, it causes problems.

It makes you more irritable, moody and less able to control your emotions. It makes it less easy to concentrate and remember stuff. It makes you clumsier and more prone to bumps, falls and accidents. And much more.

So yeah, if you lose too much sleep, you'll regret it.

'OK, SLEEP IS IMPORTANT. BUT WHY CAN'T I GET ENOUGH OF IT?'

Unfortunately, during your teens, your sleep becomes more chaotic. We all tend to have certain sleep patterns and rhythms. For example, you may regularly feel tired by 10 p.m., fall asleep by 11 p.m. and wake up at 7 a.m. Everyone's sleep patterns are subtly different, but they are all largely controlled by hormones, which are chemical signals in your body. Puberty basically means 'filling your body full of hormones', and that's what happens as you become a teenager. These hormones throw your sleep out of whack, so you get tired at different, inconvenient times.[109]

109. Usually, much later than when you were younger. For example, if you used to fall asleep at 9 p.m., now it'll be 11 p.m., 12 a.m, or even later.

At the same time, your young person's brain is doing so much developing, and you need *more* sleep so your brain can recover from the extra workload. But between the demands of parents, school and the world around us, you rarely ever *get* this extra sleep.

When you're in this sleep-deprived state of being irritable, grumpy, clumsy, emotional, forgetful, unfocused and exhausted, it would be a bad idea to keep making you wake up early, learn multiple complicated things, do many physical activities, constantly get criticized and told what to do, and be surrounded by countless others who are as irritable as you.

But that's *exactly* what school makes you do.

'THAT'S WHY SCHOOL IS SO STRESSFUL?'

One reason, sure.

Basically, some genius from the past decided it should be *the law* that the most sleep-deprived young people must wake up early and go and do many things that are

much harder when you've not had enough sleep. And everyone just nodded in agreement. Classic adults.

Let's not blame teachers for this, though. They don't make the rules about when school starts; they just deal with the consequences. And having to teach grumpy, unfocused teens?[110] I doubt that's a highlight of the job.

But there's one thing that many teachers agree has made young students get even less sleep than usual.

'LET ME GUESS . . . PHONES?'

Yeah. At this point, it would be weird if it was anything else.

While phones didn't create the problem of young people not getting enough sleep (that's largely the fault of all the biological brain stuff I described[111]), phones have definitely made it worse.

---

110. It's worth noting that you won't be exhausted and moody all the time. Most young people pick up eventually. It just takes more time and effort than it should!
111. I explained this in more depth in my previous book, *Why Your Parents Are Driving You Up The Wall And What To Do About It.*

'HOW DO PHONES MAKE US SLEEP LESS?'

Phones mess up your sleep in a few different ways.

The most obvious way is by beaming light in your eyes. When you're reading or watching stuff on your phone, the light from the screen is disrupting your sleep patterns without you realizing.

At this point, you're probably thinking:

> MY PARENTS AND TEACHERS TELL ME IT'S FINE TO READ A BOOK BEFORE BED. WHY IS READING A BOOK OK, BUT READING FROM MY PHONE IS NOT?

'I WASN'T THINKING THAT . . . BUT I AM NOW!'

Exactly.

Long story short, a book is *reflecting* light, coming from the bulb in your lamp or room light. This light hits the page, then bounces off into your eyeballs.

But the screens on phones produce *their own* light. Which makes a difference because of physics and biology. It means the light from screens is **stronger**, brighter, **harsher**.

And our eyes and brains have to work harder to cope with it. And they get worn out more, hence we get eye strain and headaches, stuff like that.

Screen light is also a combination of all different wavelengths, which are essentially *colours*. And blue light in particular, when it enters your eyes, slows down the release of melatonin, a hormone produced by your brain.

The more melatonin in your body, the sleepier you are. But if you slow down its release, it means less melatonin in your body. Which means you get tired later than you normally would if you had normal amounts of melatonin.

So too much blue light **disrupts your sleep**.

'WHY DOES BLUE LIGHT DO THAT?'

It's an evolutionary thing. The daytime sky is blue, so our ancient human brains evolved to think:

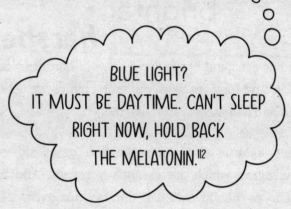

BLUE LIGHT?
IT MUST BE DAYTIME. CAN'T SLEEP
RIGHT NOW, HOLD BACK
THE MELATONIN.[112]

It's a well-known issue, though. That's why all modern phones have a blue light filter, which adjusts the screen output, so what you're looking at is made up of more 'warm' colours, meaning less blue light, which tends to be brighter and harsher.

112. If you've ever been jet-lagged, this is why. You're in a different time zone, so it's light when your body and brain expect it to be night. This scrambles your sleep patterns, leaving you fogged and confused.

'IF ALL PHONES HAVE THESE BLUE LIGHT FILTERS, WHY DO TEACHERS AND PARENTS STILL SAY MY PHONE KEEPS ME AWAKE?'

Because blue light's not the *only* issue. Phones have other ways of preventing you from sleeping.

One important thing to consider is that we can sort of *override* sleep, by which I mean if we feel something more important than sleep is happening right now, we can delay it.

Granted, the *need* for sleep doesn't go away; it just means you'll rack up 'sleep debt'. If you need, say, nine hours of sleep per night (a normal amount for someone your age), but thanks to going to bed late and waking up early for school, you only get five, you technically owe your brain and body four hours of sleep. So you are in sleep debt.

And you'll need to pay off this debt eventually, *especially* if you keep adding to it. And the longer you go without repaying your sleep debt, the harder it gets to think and function normally.

Sleep requires key parts of our brain to sort of power **down**, while excitement causes those same brain bits to power **up**.

Which, of course, makes going to sleep much harder. It's like if you're trying to shut down a computer but keep opening programs while doing so. It confuses the whole process.

Your phone connects you to everyone you know and everything going on in the world, so the odds of finding something exciting and interesting that keeps you awake are pretty high.

'WHAT SORT OF THINGS ARE WE TALKING ABOUT?'

Basically, our brains react strongly to *novelty*. By which I mean *newness*.

Not *everything* new is good, of course. A lot of new stuff is weird and off-putting. Like strange, unfamiliar foods. The sort of thing your parents will ask you to try, because you might like it, but you never do.

But if it's a new example of something we *know we like*, such as a sequel to a favourite movie or video game or a new track by our favourite artist, then it can be very enticing.

The attraction of the new is powerful. That's why we binge TV shows we like or videos from our favourite YouTuber or struggle to put down books we're really engrossed in. They keep providing us with new examples of things we're already enjoying. And these are all things our phone gives us easy acccss to, without us ever having to get out of bed. This means it's hard to resist the thought:

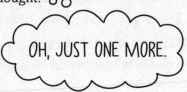

OH, JUST ONE MORE.

Even though the clock is ticking and yet another school day is getting closer and closer.

'SO I SHOULD JUST AVOID DOING ANYTHING I LIKE BEFORE BED? TYPICAL.'

Actually, you should avoid *stimulating* things. As in, things that excite us,[113] make us more 'active' or want to *do* things. For example, a good video game is stimulating because it excites us and makes us *want* to play it.

However, not all stimulation is good. Unpleasant, negative, scary things can be very stimulating indeed.

Thanks to 24-hour news, social media feeds, cameras all over the place and everywhere being connected to everywhere else, it's very quick and easy to find *something* to worry about with your phone. Whether it's a major disaster in another country, gloomy climate updates or whatever. We're spoiled for choice.

This is bad for sleep because your brain focuses more on negative, worrying things than it does on the fun stuff. It's a basic survival instinct, developed over many millions of years in the wild: when it comes to staying

---

113. Usually (but not always) in an emotional sense.

alive, the vicious tiger running towards you is probably more important than the tasty berries on a nearby bush. This has left us humans with a strong tendency to focus more on the negatives than the positives.

Unfortunately, our modern brains have taken this a bit far. When faced with almost anything unpleasant, it will think about it as a possible threat. The parts of our brain that deal with responding to threats can't really tell the difference between 'oncoming tiger' and 'worrying news story that might affect me one day, maybe'.[114] This means we often feel like we have to 'get to the bottom' of something worrying, so we can be sure whether we should be concerned about it.

And so we tend to get sucked into negative, scary stories or issues when we should be sleeping.

114. That's why anxiety is so common.

Ever heard of 'doomscrolling'? If not, look it up. But this is why it's so common.

'SO IF WE FINISH A SERIES OR BOOK OR GET TO THE BOTTOM OF SOMETHING, *THEN* WE CAN SLEEP?'

Yes, but how long is that going to take? And that's all time when you could, *should*, be sleeping.

But that's another thing our brains dislike: leaving things unfinished. Studies have been done that show that if you *pay* people to perform a task, like completing a puzzle, but tell them they can go before they're done, most people will stay and finish the puzzle, purely because they want to. Our brains don't like incompleteness.

Unfortunately, our phones provide us with many things that are very stimulating (in a good or bad way), offer constant novelty and provide experiences that *never end*. Like, is it possible to 'complete' TikTok or Instagram? Of course not. Which makes them *very* absorbing, very compelling and very good at *keeping you awake*.

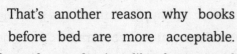 That's another reason why books before bed are more acceptable. They have clear end points, like chapters and sections, making it easier to put it down when tired. And also, the book you're reading doesn't keep tempting you with a whole new story or plot twist every six seconds.

When you're told to put your phones and devices down at least an hour before bed, it's not just due to paranoid parents worrying about screen time. It also helps prevent you getting sucked into anything that will keep you up until 2 a.m. when you've got school the next day.

'WHAT IF I'M NOT WATCHING ANYTHING, I'M JUST CHATTING WITH MY FRIENDS. IS THAT OK?'

Unfortunately, that can actually be *worse*. Even teachers are concerned about that.

Before phones, school was still hard work and stressful, but at least there was a clear separation between school and home. If there was some issue or problem between you and your friends, or something you were all obsessing over, it had to end at the school gates and be picked up the next day or after the weekend.

Sometimes this meant a time out, where everyone got to calm down about things. But actually, it usually meant people lost interest and moved on to something else.

Now, though, everyone has a phone. So whatever everyone was talking about during the day can continue in group chats and messages.

And when you're talking with friends in the group chat, when does that discussion end?

'WELL . . . WHEN EVERYONE STOPS MESSAGING?'

Right. But that might not happen for hours and hours. It just takes one night owl to keep things rolling.

Remember how stimulating we find interacting and socializing? How we dislike things being unfinished?

How we like new things? A friendly, open-ended group chat can be all that. So is it any wonder it'll keep you awake and engaged?

Teachers have picked up on this, apparently, thanks to so many students turning up at school more exhausted than ever because they were up all night talking to their friends with their phones.

And it's not a simple matter of 'put the phone down' in this case. A discussion isn't like a book, movie or TV show; you can't just pick up where you left off, hours later. It *keeps going*, even if you're not part of it. And this is important.

Teachers tell me of young people with stricter parents who have a **'no phones after 8 p.m.'** rule. So they tend to get more sleep than their friends. Which you'd think would make school easier for them, right?

Ah, but then they get to school, having missed all the hours of chat and interaction their friends were having, into the night with their phones. So they're excluded, cut-off from their friend group. And this can make us feel rejected and lonely. Something which, as we've seen, stresses us out, *especially* at your age.

It becomes a balancing act: sleep or acceptance? Which one do you need more of to get through the school day without too much stress? It's a tricky question to answer, but one phones force you to think about.

'IS THERE ANYTHING WE CAN *DO* ABOUT THIS?'

In a sense, yes.

Some schools in the US have tried starting an hour later for teenage students to give them more time to sleep. They found that grades improved, behaviour was better and there were less problems overall. So clearly even a little bit of extra sleep goes a long way at your age.

There doesn't seem to be any sign that schools in general are going to do the same any time soon, though. Hopefully they'll come round eventually, but it'll be a while.

In the meantime, it probably *is* a good idea **to disengage from your phone before you go to sleep**.

Much of what parents and teachers say may be suspect, but not this.

You can make it easier for yourself too by putting your phone in a separate room or at least out of sight and arm's reach. Even a tiny bit of extra effort can make an already tired brain say:

OH, FORGET IT!

and go to sleep.

Sure, you might miss out on the group chat, but it's often easier, and healthier, to catch up on the gossip than the sleep you've lost.

'THIS WOULD MEAN I NEVER DO ANYTHING I ACTUALLY *LIKE*, THOUGH.'

Fair point. In a way, schools and teachers often need to take a look in the mirror here. On the one hand, they're wagging their finger at you because you spend so much time on your phone instead of sleeping.

On the other hand, they're regularly saying:

> HERE ARE SEVERAL HOURS OF EXTRA WORK AND REVISION YOU NEED TO DO AT HOME, IN YOUR OWN TIME. AND IF YOU DON'T DO IT, YOU'LL BE IN TROUBLE!

In this case, can you really be blamed for wanting some time to enjoy yourself, no matter how late it is? If your school and teachers don't care about your sleep unless it affects them, well, they can deal with you being groggy. It's only fair, right?

'THAT'S WHAT I HEARD!'

Here's an interesting thing: teachers are often *more* worried about the risks and dangers of phones than parents tend to be.[115]

Which is odd. Because you'd think that parents would be the more concerned ones. They're directly responsible for you and your well-being at all times, until you're an adult yourself.

Meanwhile, teachers only have to deal with you for a few hours a day at most. So why would they get so het up about what your phone is or isn't doing to you?

Of course that's not how it works. There's much more going on.

---

115. In fairness, a lot of teachers are *also* parents. But let's keep those things separate for now, just to make things easy.

When it comes to looking out for young people, your parents may be directly responsible for you (and your siblings, if you have any), but that's usually it.

But your teachers? They're responsible for your entire class, even if it's only for an hour. Which usually means dozens of young people, many of whom aren't that keen on being there (or grumpy and irritable through lack of sleep), all forced to sit together in a room and learn about conjugated verbs or whatever.

And they have to do this with lots of different classes, several times a day.

What I'm getting at is, your parents are focused on looking after a small number of young people (you, maybe your siblings), but teachers? Teachers have to deal with them in groups.

And when you put a lot of young people together like this, there'll always be *some* friction, which leads to bickering, arguments, insults, etc. Issues that teachers end up having to sort out.

But when you add phones into the mix, it can make matters a whole lot worse in ways that teachers struggle to deal with.

'HOW DO PHONES MAKE THINGS WORSE, EXACTLY?'

Well, consider this.

In your school, have you ever experienced a student or group of students spreading some ridiculous rumour about another student? It's incredibly common.[116] And even if it starts from a grain of truth, it quickly becomes something else entirely. Something *not* true, to be precise.

For instance, say our old friend Jimmy Gibberish happened to have a bit of toilet paper stuck to his shoe. It wasn't even *his* toilet paper, just some dropped by someone else that he stepped on without knowing it. It happens.

---

[116]. It happened to me a few times, like when people said I had nits and that they were my pets and I gave them all names. For the record, I *didn't* have nits. Even at that age, I barely had hair!

But then another student, one who's maybe sick of the nonsense stories Jimmy tells all the time, sees this and has a chuckle to themselves. And they tell their friend, who laughs. And they tell everyone they sit by in the next lesson. Who tell their friends at lunchtime. And so on.

But you know how it is. As it spreads, people add details to make it funnier (or meaner) and things get twisted. What started with Jimmy having a bit of toilet paper on his shoe ends up with multiple people being told that Jimmy had a very unfortunate, and 'explosive', accident that morning and had to leg it to the bathroom to deal with it.

'GROSS!'

I know. But if you've never heard any jokes or comments like this, then you must go to a *very* unusual school.

Anyway, now Jimmy has lots of people mocking him for something that never happened. Whatever he might have done, that's harsh.

What would usually happen then is that a teacher, hearing about this, would have stern words with whichever group or class is spreading these rumours, maybe threatening detention if they keep at it. Nine times out of ten, that would be it. Everyone goes home at the end of the day, and next morning everyone's moved on to something else.

Now imagine the same thing happens but everyone's got a phone. In this case, the student who saw Jimmy with the toilet paper on his shoe took a photo of it and posted it, along with several laugh-cry emojis, in a group chat with all their friends. Or the entire school *year. Or the whole school!* Maybe it was airdropped to a general shared file? Every school now has its own way of sharing things, I hear. I don't know, I'm old!

The point is, within five minutes, *everyone* is laughing at Jimmy. Sure, the ridiculous stuff about the explosive accident hasn't had time to develop into a rumour, which is a good thing. But ask yourself what you'd prefer: a few people laughing at you about something that didn't happen, or *everyone* laughing at you about something that *did*! That there's a photo of!

'BUT A BIT OF TOILET PAPER ON A SHOE SURELY ISN'T *THAT* EMBARRASSING?'

I'll make you a deal. If you can tell me that nobody in your school has ever been mercilessly roasted for the most minor thing, I'll agree with you.

'OK, FAIR POINT.'

Yeah. You young people are great in many ways. But you can be *brutal*.

Anyway, the point is, thanks to phones, Jimmy's reputation at school, and therefore his confidence, has been seriously knocked. And at your age this can be a big deal, making you feel sad, anxious, isolated and other things that are bad for mental well-being.

But what's a teacher meant to do about this? It's their job to fix it, but it happened so fast they probably weren't even aware of it until too late. And how do they respond? Give *the whole school* detention? I can't see that going down well.

Thanks to phones, this could happen to any student, at any time, and teachers are pretty much powerless to do anything about it. And when you're in charge of dozens of headstrong young people, being seen to be powerless makes your job much harder. Have you ever had a classic nervous substitute teacher? One who was obviously so anxious and unsure about what they were doing they completely lost control of the class? If so, you'll know what I'm talking about.

And that's only when students aren't doing this sort of thing (using their phones to mock and tease others) *on purpose*. Because sometimes, they are.

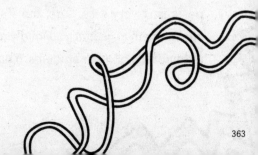

'THAT'S *BULLYING*, ISN'T IT?'

It absolutely would be.

You've probably heard it called *cyberbullying*.

And it's something parents and teachers are very concerned about.

Some would say it's not as bad as 'real' bullying, by which they mean the face-to-face kind. It *is*, though.

Sure, with in-person bullying, the risk of physical violence is a big part of it. Some hulking lump with more biceps than brain cells looming over you, promising to do very painful things to you. That's obviously going to be a deeply unpleasant experience, even if they *don't* go through with it.

And, for all the reasons we've discussed already, being mocked, criticised and humiliated in person will have more impact than if it happens via a screen. Having a load of school friends add angry faces on your online posts isn't very nice, sure, but it's surely not as bad as having them all jeer at you loudly across the yard in front of hundreds of other students. That can be *mortifying*.

However, while physical bullying is bad, it's the *emotional* impact that can be most harmful. Young people get knocked and injured all the time and can just shrug it off. Which is something we adults, who often injure ourselves just by getting out of bed too quickly, are quite jealous of.

But if the physical injuries you suffer lead to emotional 'injuries', like feelings of inferiority, rejection, mockery and low status, like what happens with physical bullying, these are all very stressful and can stay with you for a long time.

And at least you can get away from face-to-face bullying. You can leave school or go to your home and stay there. This doesn't *fix* anything, sure, but it provides safety for a bit.

Not with cyberbullying, though. If you've got your phone, and your bullies have theirs, they can keep harassing you, insulting you, criticising you and generally attacking you through your messages, your social media accounts . . . All from the convenience of their own home.

'YOU COULD DELETE ALL YOUR ACCOUNTS AND SET EVERYTHING TO PRIVATE?'

You could. And people do. But how much of your life is connected to what you do online? If you suddenly 'went dark', think of how much you'd miss out on. You couldn't interact with anyone who *doesn't* bully you. You'd not be able to see photos of what your friends and community are up to or share yours with them. You'd miss out on the latest happenings and have to hear about them second or third hand, much later.

It's like hiding in your house *and never leaving*, purely to avoid in-person bullying.

Sure, it keeps you safe, but . . . at what cost?

'WELL, YOU CAN SAVE ANY OF THE NASTY MESSAGES OR POSTS WITH SCREENGRABS IF THEY DELETE THEM. THEN YOU'VE GOT PROOF.'

Now you're thinking! That's one of the few 'advantages' of cyberbullying. It leaves a clear trail.

Someone spreading a nasty rumour about you can't really say, 'Well, that's what *I* heard!' when their phone shows them sending the messages that started it.

Of course messages can be deleted. Posts can be taken down. But like you say, you can take screengrabs just in case. But the bully can say you Photoshopped those. And so on. And so on.

The thing is, though, even if all that works, it still means it's up to the *victim* to deal with it. They need to save and keep the hurtful, horrible stuff on their phone 'just in case'. Looking at it can make you sad, upset or anxious all over again. But at the same time, it can be hard to *avoid* looking at it, just like how it's hard to avoid picking a scab or poking a broken tooth with your tongue.

Basically, it's saying to bullying victims,

CAN'T YOU DEAL WITH IT YOURSELF?

Which, you know, isn't great.

'SO HOW *ARE* WE MEANT TO RESPOND TO CYBERBULLYING?'

Well, when bullying happens in school, the advice is

'Tell a teacher'.

For the record, that's still the right approach and you should definitely do that if you find yourself the target of bullies.

However, once again, if phones are involved, everything gets more complicated.

Like, how are teachers meant to stop students sending messages with their own phones? Are they even allowed to do that? Same applies if it happens outside of school hours: is it even any of a teacher's business? Many would say yes, but it's not as clear-cut as you'd hope.

In fact, if harassment happens online through your phones, how's a teacher even meant to see it? If a teacher tried to add you on Snapchat or follow you on TikTok, that would be . . . weird. It's bad enough bumping into a teacher in the supermarket; you don't want them liking your Instagram posts! Most young people, *and* their parents, would find that rather worrying.

There are good reasons for this, and most teachers would happily agree with them. Like how teachers are expected, even required, to maintain a personal boundary between themselves and you to ensure they keep a sense of authority and treat all students as fairly as they can.

Connecting with teachers online would really confuse matters here. Not least because it's hard to accept being told off by someone you know has a cat called Tinkleface. So teachers and students rarely mix online.

It does mean, though, that bullying can happen in part of the virtual world that teachers can't access. But . . . it's still their job to do something about it.

By now, it's hopefully clear why teachers might have more of a grudge against phones than your average parent.

'YEAH, BUT WHAT DO THEY WANT US TO DO? GET RID OF OUR PHONES?'

To be honest, I bet some teachers genuinely *would* like that. Although I doubt they actually expect it to happen.

But in order to understand this issue a bit better, let's have a look at the bigger picture.

When grown adults find themselves involved in hassles or drama caused by other adults, it's common for them to say,

IT'S LIKE BEING BACK IN SCHOOL![117]

117. Or 'It's like high school all over again!', if you're American.

Someone in the office spreads gossip about a co-worker?

> IT'S LIKE BEING BACK IN SCHOOL!

A member of a friend group has a bad break-up with another member and makes everyone take a side?

> IT'S LIKE BEING BACK IN SCHOOL!

And despite all those 'best days of your life' comments about school, parents and adults do *not* mean this is a good thing. (Adults being inconsistent? Whatever next!)

What they're saying is that school was a time when arguments, rivalries, emotional outbursts, backstabbing and unreasonable competitiveness – basically the sorts of things that would lead to bullying or spreading rumours about someone – were all common. Because everyone was so young and didn't know any better.

As an adult, you're meant to leave all that childishness behind.

'THAT'S ACTUALLY PRETTY INSULTING!'

It is, isn't it?

Is it *fair*, though? No, it's not.

While many adults seem to think the way you behave in school is something you grow out of, it's probably fairer to say that how young people behave in school *is just how people are!*

When enough human beings are put together in one place, they'll always end up being competitive, judgemental, emotional, gossipy and all that stuff. It's how we're wired.

Sure, we want to be social and have friends, but we also want to be liked, respected and admired. And we want to be *right*. And if everyone wants this, it quickly leads to arguments, misleading people to get them on your side, making yourself look good by making others look bad and so on.

When we get older, we just get better at controlling this and keeping such thoughts and impulses to ourselves.

And school's where we learn to explore what sort of behaviour is acceptable and what we can say or do **without causing serious upset or ending important relationships.**

Basically, you learn a lot more in school than just what teachers tell you in lessons. It's not all about textbooks and equations.

It's another reason why school is so important. Figuring out how to deal and get along with others is a tricky thing. Luckily, it all happens in the *normally* safe environment of school.[118] It takes place away from your parents, so you can figure this stuff out yourself, which is important so you learn how to do it as an independent adult. But there are also teachers around, who can step in where needed and steer you in the right direction.

And that's the issue. Teachers have always had to deal with all the conflicts and tensions and bickering and misbehaviours and emotional outbursts that happen

---

118. This is not to dismiss those who have a hard, or even traumatic, time at school, which happens depressingly often. But that's a whole other issue.

when enough young people are forced together in one place. And it's a difficult job.

As a result, schools have built up numerous rules, boundaries, expectations and codes of conduct, which mean that teachers have established ways of dealing with tricky or troublesome behaviours.

They didn't always *work*, sure. But they were there. There was a system in place.

But now you all have phones, which, for teachers, has made everything much more complicated. The boundaries between everybody involved, and between inside and outside of school, are much blurrier. Everyone is now connected 24/7 online.

So you can't really blame them for getting stressed about, and resentful of, phones.

Sure, teachers get very stressed out by phones and how they affect things in school. But . . . do you?

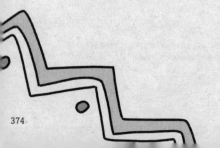

'ME? NOT REALLY. I GUESS IT'S NEVER OCCURRED TO ME.'

Exactly. If my experience is anything to go by, actual young people, like yourself, tend to be a lot less bothered about the whole thing. Which makes sense, when you think about it.

While teachers are having to adjust to the presence of phones, which is difficult and stressful for them, you don't have to do that. Phones have always been there, as far as you're concerned.

Basically, from the point of view of teachers, phones have created a 'new normal' in schools. Just like how the Covid pandemic quickly made staying indoors and virtual learning normal for everyone, phones have made a totally new way of doing things in schools 'normal'.

It means the old rules and expectations are no longer enough, and teachers are doing all they can to adapt to it, to figure out how phones affect concentration, bullying, discipline and many other things like that. All for the sake of your education, safety and well-being. Because that's their job.

But to you, phones aren't a 'new normal'. **They're just regular old normal.**

If anything, you probably figured out how phones are best used in schools before your teachers did. Maybe that's one thing teachers can learn from you?

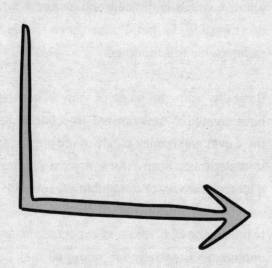

'GLORIFIED BABYSITTERS!'

So you've got your parents moaning about your phone at home and your teachers doing it in school. It can sometimes feel like they're ganging up on you.

However, that's not the case. Because, strange as it may seem, parents and teachers regularly disagree on things. As often (if not *more* often) as they agree.

This isn't unusual. And even if they don't agree on things, parents and teachers usually just put up with each other, for the most part.

But if there's one thing that's led to even more clashes between them, it's phones. In fact, when issues concerning phones crop up, teachers can often be more irked by your parents than by you.

'HANG ON, GO BACK A SECOND. WHY DO PARENTS AND TEACHERS DISAGREE SO MUCH?'

Because of you, basically.

'ME?? WHAT DID I DO?'

Oh, you didn't do anything (as far as I know). You just, sort of, exist. Which is absolutely not your fault, by the way.

But remember when I explained how parents are responsible for their specific children, while teachers are responsible for dozens at once? This means parents and teachers have very different things that they consider to be most important.

Your parents' main concern is raising you, providing for you and protecting you and your well-being. That's the point of being a parent, for most.[119] They want the

---

119. Sadly, not every parent feels this way, and their children end up having much tougher lives because of it.

best for you, and usually object to anything that could potentially harm you and your development.

These concerns might often be *wrong* or very annoying, but they do technically come from a good place. So that's something, right?

Now, teachers – their job is not to raise and provide for you. It's to get your whole class[120] to learn everything you need to learn, in the time they have, and to pass whatever exams or assessments are at the end of it. They basically have to supervise, educate and generally look out for lots of young people at once.

This can be very demanding, even chaotic. Does Student A need more help? Should Student B be moved away from their boisterous, bad-influence friends? Does smart Student C need help or is it better to let them carry on as they are?

120. Or, if we're being realistic, as many of your class as possible.

Of course, if it was up to your parents, your teacher would spend most of their time with *you*, to provide you with the best education. But then the parents of every other student will want the same for their child. Which means teachers are expected to provide one-to-one education to dozens of students at the same time? How's *that* meant to work?

Basically, if teachers did what parents wanted, they'd literally be unable to do their job.

So teachers and parents end up disagreeing.

'SO WHO'S ACTUALLY *RIGHT*: MY PARENTS OR MY TEACHERS?'

I wish there was a better answer than 'it depends', but . . . it depends.

Sometimes parents are right, sometimes teachers are. Sometimes they're both wrong.

For instance, it shouldn't happen, but sometimes teachers do treat students unfairly. Which is wrong.

That's what 'unfair' means.

It can be something simple. Like if other students are making a noise nearby, but your teacher mistakenly blames you, so *you* get punished. Which is infuriating.

It can be something less obvious. Sometimes certain students are constantly disruptive or need a lot of help, so the teacher focuses mostly on them. But other students, like yourself, still need *some* help. But you get overlooked due to those who need more (and may be quite loud about it). Which, again, isn't fair.

Sometimes a teacher simply dislikes a student for some reason.[121] This absolutely should not happen, but teachers are only human, so it can. But it's still unfair.

In examples like this, and others you've probably experienced yourself, teachers are in the wrong. But you, the student, can't really do much about it.

But your parents can. If you're not receiving fair treatment in school, your parents can stick up for you and try to sort the issues out. They'd usually *want* to. And they'd be right to do so.

121. Sometimes teachers are just jerks.

'SO PARENTS SHOULD HAVE THE FINAL SAY ON THINGS?'

In situations like what I just described, sure. Parents absolutely should get involved with teachers and school issues when needed, when things are affecting you, especially if it's unfairly.

But the words 'when needed' are key. Because many parents like to get involved when they *aren't* needed. You're their child, so they feel they should have a say over what happens to you in school. Only, when they do that, they can often make things much worse for you. Or your teachers.

'HOW DO MY PARENTS MAKE THINGS *WORSE*?'

Whatever you think of teachers, teaching is a demanding, difficult job. It's also a very important job because you're in charge of *other people's children* and their education. That's a big deal!

But many parents genuinely believe they know what's

best when it comes to teaching. This often makes them dismissive towards teachers and all that they do, calling them things like 'glorified babysitters'. Meaning, they don't really *do* anything beyond keep an eye on a bunch of kids to stop them misbehaving or hurting themselves.[122]

On top of that, we've seen how parents can be a bit . . . shall we say, overprotective? But some go completely overboard and try to protect their child from anything negative *at all*. This includes bad marks or any form of criticism. Which are hard to avoid in any normal school.

Alternatively, some parents are so protective they refuse to even consider the very idea that their child might be less than perfect.

Many teachers have horror stories about such parents. Like that time Verity got a poor mark for biology on her report card, which resulted in an outraged Mr and Mrs Booglesnap storming down to the school for a blazing row with the biology teacher, who *clearly* wasn't doing her job!

---

122. Although, if you've done some babysitting yourself, you'll know this is offensive to both teachers *and* babysitters. Anyone who regularly babysits *30 kids at once* is a hero, not lazy.

The fact that Verity got a bad mark because she hates biology and refuses to study? That never crosses her parents' minds. And they wouldn't accept it if it did.

So yeah, as well as an already demanding job, teachers often have to endure parents telling them they're doing it wrong. When they're often not. If anything, the *parents* are doing their job wrong. Because basically wrapping your child in a protective cocoon, where nothing negative can get at them and they never experience anything challenging or unpleasant, does no good for anyone.

'YIKES! HOW DO TEACHERS AND PARENTS MANAGE IF THEY HATE EACH OTHER SO MUCH?'

OK, I may have overdone it there.

While you'll always get some exceptions, in most cases parents and teachers are very reasonable and get along fine. Even if they don't 100 per cent agree, they try to work things out reasonably.

But the thing is, even when parents and teachers didn't see eye-to-eye, it wasn't *that* big an issue in the past. There was always a clear divide between them. When a young person was in school, teachers were in charge. Anywhere else, parents were ultimately in control.

Parents may not have *liked* not having any control of what went on with you during school,[123] much like they don't like not knowing everything you're doing with your phone. But they still had to accept that their influence over you ended at the school gates, and only a genuine emergency, like you being ill or injured, would change that.

In this set-up, everyone knew where they stood at least.

But it's different now. Things are much more confused. Thanks to phones.

123. Which affected your relationship with them, also something else I covered at length in my previous book.

'HOW HAVE PHONES MADE THINGS MORE CONFUSING?'

Well, let me ask you this: do your parents ever contact you when you're in school, through your phone?

'YEAH, OF COURSE.'

And you're OK with that?

'WELL, YEAH. WHY WOULDN'T I BE?'

Fair enough. Most of the young people I spoke to when writing this felt pretty much the same.

But for adults like me, and many teachers, this *is* weird.

Before, if your parents wanted to speak to you when you were in school, they had to call the school office[124] and tell them who they needed to contact and what year and class you were in.

124. Or front desk, or whatever it is your school has.

It was a long-winded process, which usually meant it was only ever used for important things. Imagine going through all that only for your mum or dad to say:

I WAS THINKING WE COULD HAVE SAUSAGES FOR DINNER. IS THAT OK WITH YOU?

This meant that your parents' influence over you in school was kept to a minimum. Which, according to many, is how it should be.

But now you've got a phone. And carry it with you at all times. Meaning your parents can contact you at any time. Which basically means your parents have more of a 'presence' in your school. And the more of a presence your parents have, the less authority your teacher has, and the harder it is for them to do their job.

Look at it this way: your timetable says you have maths first thing, then music. So you finish maths, leave the maths classroom and head to the music room. But halfway through the music lesson . . . your maths teacher wanders in, comes up to you and starts talking to you about geometry and statistics.

You wouldn't be OK with this, right? It would be confusing and disruptive. And it would *certainly* annoy the heck out of your music teacher. Because your maths teacher has strayed beyond their teaching time and into someone else's.

Teachers can feel this way about parents messaging your phone while you're meant to be learning. In fact, your phone leads to teachers and parents butting heads surprisingly often.

But if your school does have a 'no phones' rule, or introduces one, there can often be a lot of resistance to this. **From *parents*.**

'EH?'

Yeah. Parents, the ones regularly moaning about you spending too much time on your phone, will often object if your teachers say to put it away.

Why? Their usual answer is:

> WHAT IF I NEED TO GET
> IN TOUCH WITH YOU?

Which they can't do if your phone is hidden away in a locker by the teacher's desk.

This means that, for all their moaning about you having a phone, it seems parents get upset at the thought of you *not* having one too.

It makes them feel better, more secure, being able to contact you whenever they like. That way they have a level of control over you, even from a distance. They can call you and say:

> COME HOME NOW!

or whatever, if they felt they needed to. This eases their worries about your safety and well-being too.

We saw the benefits of this earlier, with how parents are more willing to let you go out to meet friends. However, some parents clearly feel the same applies to school;

you're not really out of their sight there either, as long as you've got your phone.

Again, though, this makes a teacher's job harder. Especially because, while teachers may tell you to put your phone away and ignore the calls and messages you're getting, what if they're coming from your *parents*? It could be a family emergency! Isn't that more important than lessons?

Or it could be a message about the sausages. You don't really know unless you *check your phone*. So your teacher's lesson is disrupted, whether it's for a valid reason or a daft one.

Basically, who's more in the right here: parents or teachers?

'PARENTS. NO . . . TEACHERS. NO, WAIT . . . I DON'T KNOW!'

See what I'm saying?

And this is when your parents aren't getting involved in

your school life by marching up to the school gates, like poor Verity's parents. Because, thanks to your phone, they can now do that easily. And it's not pretty.

For instance, imagine you have a falling out with your friends because one of them says or does something meant 'as a joke'. Whatever, you're hurt and upset. Normally, you'd maybe tell a teacher or hang out with some different friends until you feel better. Or they apologize. Or you all just decide to ignore it. In most cases, it'll all work out in the end.

But what happens if, while you're still upset, your parents check in via your phone and ask why you seem down. And you tell them:

> OH, JIMMY GIBBERISH SAID *THE HURTFUL THING*.

Most parents would try to console or reassure you. But some might just go, as they say, absolutely nuclear!

Maybe they call the school directly, demanding justice. Or message Jimmy's parents or the whole parent group chat,[125] calling Jimmy a loathsome ratbag and his parents' neglectful monsters or worse. They might even contact Jimmy himself. Or his parents do, to have a go at him, after *your* parents have had a go at *them*.

Your parents may mean well, and the urge to defend your child can be very powerful, but they haven't *helped* here, have they? At first, just you were upset. Now everyone is upset with everyone else!

They've just created a much bigger mess all round. One your teachers now have to deal with. All thanks to phones.

'BUT WHAT DO YOU WANT ME TO DO? BLOCK MY PARENTS?'

Would that be so bad?

125. Most parents regularly keep in touch with your friends' parents to discuss school matters or just to socialize. You're not the only one with a phone, remember.

Actually, ignore that. That'll get us both in trouble.

But if your parents are the sort who will try to get involved in your school life through your phone, you should at least consider having a discussion about this and why it's not helpful and they shouldn't do it.

After all, your parents probably expect *you* to be respectful and polite by not using your phone in certain situations. Or not to contact *them* at work unless it's an emergency.

Well, this works both ways, and the same applies to you. In school, *you're* busy learning. Most parents get pretty mad if you fail to do that! But it's a lot harder to do with your parents virtually breathing down your neck.

They have to let you do your own thing at some point. If not in school, then where?

Your teachers will thank you if nothing else.

And you can agree on sausages for dinner at the end of the school day. They don't take *that* long to cook!

CHAPTER 6

MOBILE
HOTSPOTS

Here we are, at the last chapter! And yet, I've still barely made a dent in the number of things I *could* have told you about.

Because phones do . . . *So. Much. Stuff!* That little glowing rectangle in your pocket is a gateway to everything humans have ever created, discovered and invented. Of *course* it'll affect you, in countless ways that are all so different.

However, despite everything we've looked at – physical health, mental health, relationships, celebrities and fandom, bullying, history, memory, home life, school life, lies and truth – there's one thing they have in common.

Once phones got involved with them, things *changed*. It's as if phones immediately say

BORING!
LET'S TRY *THIS*!

With that in mind, there are a few more things that phones have 'thrown out of whack'. Things that are very important. Things that will almost certainly affect you at some point, if they haven't already. And your parents too, probably.

So, to finish off, let's take a look at these important things that phones have made all confusing so you can be ready for them, when you're affected. Or understand them better, if that's already happened.

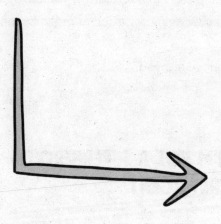

'CHECK YOUR PRIVACY SETTINGS.'

Do you live two separate lives?

Just to be clear, I'm not asking if you are Spider-Man or a deep-cover agent for a secret organization.

Although . . . are you?

'NO, I'M NOT A SUPERHERO OR A SECRET AGENT.'

Ah, shame. But never mind.

What I meant was, some people are actually very different online compared to how they are in the real world. Maybe you're quiet and shy in real life, but a superstar in the making on Insta. Maybe you struggle to come up with anything good to say in person but are notorious for your epic burns and quick comebacks in the group chat.

Or maybe there's not much difference at all between how you are online and how you are in person.

'YEAH, IT'S PROBABLY THAT LAST ONE.'

Not surprising, really. You're still young, still developing, figuring out the kind of person you are, what you like, what you believe in. Your identity, basically. It would be a bit much for you to have to develop two separate identities, especially with everything else you're having to deal with.

Having real-world and online identities was probably more of a thing in the 'old days' (i.e. 20 years ago), when you could only get online with a desktop computer or laptop, maybe connected to an actual broadband cable, like a caveman. This meant you could focus on real-world stuff *or* online stuff. Doing both at the same time was really tricky.

That's not a problem now, though, thanks to phones. Now the digital world is just a swipe away at all times; it can get our attention 24/7, with alerts and notifications. And thanks to cameras and video sharing, whatever we're doing in the real world can become digital content in a matter of minutes. So yeah, thanks to phones the real world and your digital world overlap more than ever.

This might seem convenient, fun even. But you still need to be careful here.

Because life in the real world and life in the digital world are still very different, **with different rules.**

And one particular concern that gets a lot of attention (ironically) from parents is your privacy.

'HOW DOES MY PHONE AFFECT MY PRIVACY? I DON'T LET ANYONE ELSE USE IT.'

Actually, you don't need anyone else to use your phone. You can end up damaging your own privacy with your phone, without anyone's help.

One important difference between the digital and real worlds is this:

What happens online **often *stays* online.**

Say you end up needing to tell a close friend something important, personal or embarrassing about yourself. If you choose to do this face-to-face in a hushed conversation in a park or their bedroom, what you've shared only exists in the memory of your friend.

But if you write it out and send it via a messenger app, well, that could easily leave a record that someone else could access and . . . do whatever they like with.

'BUT IT'S A PRIVATE MESSAGE BETWEEN ME AND A FRIEND I TRUST. SURELY THAT'S FINE?'

You might think so. You might even be right. Good friends share personal details and secrets all the time. That's one of the best things about *having* friends.

But even the best of friends can still fall out. This can happen at any age, but you're still young. You and your friend are still dealing with powerful emotions and too little sleep. It's *very* common for people your age to argue and fall out, even temporarily. And if this does happen to you, your friend, or possibly *ex*-friend, has got a written record of some deeply personal details about you.

And if they wanted to screengrab and share that far and wide? Well, you won't even know until it's too late. Remember Jimmy and the toilet paper?[126]

---

126. I know I made that up, but there are plenty of examples of it happening for real online . . . which suggests *another* breach of privacy.

But even if the friend you sent the message to is 100 per cent trustworthy, did you use a messenger service you programmed yourself? And did you set up your own personal internet to run it on?

'I DON'T HAVE A CLUE HOW TO DO ANY OF THAT!'

No doubt. If you did, it would be scarily impressive.

Many parents worry about exactly this sort of thing, though.

We all use messenger apps and internet connections. Our phones depend on them. But such things are made and provided by companies run by people we have absolutely no clue about. So there are countless complete strangers who could, in theory, be building a record of everything you've ever put online.

'OK, SO I SHOULD KEEP PRIVATE CHATS FACE-TO-FACE. THAT'S NOT SO BAD.'

That probably is a good idea, but it won't solve everything. Most of what you do and say online *isn't* meant to be private. If you've got Instagram or TikTok or whatever, the whole point is sharing yourself, and your content, with others.

Which is fun and rewarding. It's human nature to want to connect and be liked, as we know.

But once you've shared your content publicly, **it's out there now.**

Even if you delete it later, who knows who's shared or saved or screengrabbed it.

'AGAIN, *WHO* WOULD DO THAT? AND WHY?'

Look, I'm not going to sugar-coat it: there are a lot of bad people out there who will use other people's information to take advantage of them.

If they have access to your personal, secret details, they can threaten to make them public or share them unless you do as they say. Basically, people can do a lot of harm to someone if they have enough personal details about them.

And such people often prefer to prey on younger people, like yourself, because you usually don't have much experience of this sort of thing. So you don't realize what's happening. In such situations, you'd ideally talk to your parents and do what they say, but we know how likely *that* is to happen.

As for what such people want to do with or to you? Let's just say, it's nothing good.

I'm not trying to scare you here (although you've probably heard worse than this in school already). And such things happen *very* rarely.

But they *do* happen. And it helps if you realize, when parents keep fretting about you using your phone, that this is the sort of thing they are seriously worried about. So practising common sense and thinking very carefully about what you do and put out online, while you're as young as you are, is something they very much want you to do.

And it's probably a good idea in general, to be honest.

'YOU KEEP MENTIONING HOW YOUNG I AM. IS THAT SUCH A BIG DEAL?'

In a sense, yes. It's why parents are as concerned as they are. And not just for the 'What if dodgy sorts try to take advantage of your inexperience?' reasons.

The thing is, parents, and all adults, remember what it was like being your age.[127] And a lot of what they

---

127. They maybe don't remember it *accurately*, as we saw in Chapter 2. But they do remember it.

remember from back then will be . . . quite embarrassing.

That's probably unavoidable. The whole point of this stage of your life is to explore and try new things, to make connections, to find out what you like and don't like, and work on who you are. Despite how many times you'll be told off or criticized by grumpy older people for it, it's important for helping you grow into the mature, independent adult you'll eventually become.

Although, as you've probably noticed, it can be a bit of a 'messy' process. Your emotions are turned up to maximum, you're not getting enough sleep, everyone's already on your case, you're experiencing totally unfamiliar feelings. And you have to deal with all this, while parents and teachers are constantly hassling you about everything.

What I'm getting at is, you *will* eventually make decisions that, when you look back at them later, you won't be proud of.

Every adult you know went through the same thing, so they'll all have memories from their teenage years that make them want to collapse on the floor in embarrassment.

So, for most adults, the idea that these embarrassing teenage experiences would be recorded and saved, and that anyone could just look them up whenever they wanted?

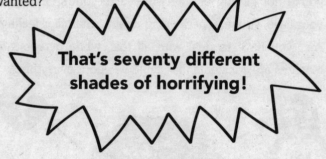

That's seventy different shades of horrifying!

And many of them are worried that this is exactly what will happen to you.

'WHY WOULD THAT HAPPEN TO ME?'

Because remember, you're going through your teenage phase *right now*. The one where you're still figuring out who you are, what you like. You'll be making these decisions and doing these things that you'll later regret and feel embarrassed about, just like your parents did.

But you have a phone.

Which means you're going to be recording a lot of what you do and sharing it online. And a lot of what you do and share will be stuff you find incredibly embarrassing later, or so parents fear.

Like, many adults will remember having a massive teen crush on someone that they now look back on as awkward and childish. The possibility that they could have recorded and uploaded a ten-minute video of a tearful rant about said crush? That anyone in the world could look up and watch, at any time? It makes them want to die from cringe!

You just don't think about this sort of thing at your age. Why would you? But your parents will try to stop you making such mistakes so you don't experience the horror yourself when *you* are their age. Only this horror won't just be remembered, it'll be *recorded*.

'AND? WHAT'S THE WORST THAT CAN HAPPEN IF SOMEONE SEES WHAT I PUT ONLINE NOW, WHEN I'M OLDER?'

That . . . is a very good question.

If anything, owning up to and embracing the embarrassing stuff you do when you're younger is often better for you than ignoring or hiding it.

It's like how if you injure a muscle in your arm or leg, it tends to get better faster if you *keep using it*. Keep it active. In healthy and safe ways, of course, like with specific exercises or stretches.

But trying to ignore it? Saying,

NOPE, THAT NEVER HAPPENED?

This often makes things *worse*. And it's the same for denying or suppressing the awkward emotional memories from your youth. They don't just go away if you ignore or deny them.

If anything, they get worse. They build up and fester, so when you finally do remember them it's like finding a lettuce that's been forgotten about in the bottom of the fridge. For four months. *Nobody* enjoys dealing with that.

Also, a grown adult, genuinely judging you for the stuff you did as a young person? That's not someone whose opinion should matter to you in any case. They clearly missed a few steps in the maturity process themselves.

'SO WHY ARE MY PARENTS SO WORRIED ABOUT THIS?'

It's probably another thing that comes from you and your parents growing up at different times. And them having a different mindset about phones and the digital world compared to you.

Their thinking is based on *memories* of their youth. Your parents can't help thinking, 'What if phones and the internet were around when I did all that embarrassing stuff? That would be mortifying!' And nothing can shake that concern because there's no way to change the past.

But phones *weren't* around at the time. And that's the key thing. If they were, your teenage parents probably *wouldn't have done the embarrassing things*. Not in the same way, at least.

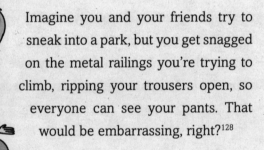

Imagine you and your friends try to sneak into a park, but you get snagged on the metal railings you're trying to climb, ripping your trousers open, so everyone can see your pants. That would be embarrassing, right?[128]

But then, one of your friends says, in all seriousness:

IMAGINE IF TWO HUNDRED PEOPLE WERE WATCHING US THEN. WOULDN'T THAT BE HUMILIATING!?

128. I asked my friend who this happened to and he said, 'Yes, it would.'

I mean, they're not wrong. But they're overlooking the most important fact. Which is, if hundreds of people were watching you, *you wouldn't have done it!* Nobody tries sneaking into a park they're not supposed to go into if 200 people are watching them. That's not how 'sneaking' works.

And the same technically applies to phones and what your parents got up to. If your parents could genuinely have said 'this might end up online' before doing embarrassing things as teens, they would probably have done something different.

'SO I SHOULDN'T WORRY TOO MUCH ABOUT MY PRIVACY WHEN I SHARE STUFF WITH MY PHONE?'

Oh no, you definitely should. For the reasons mentioned just now, like the risks of having your private confessions screengrabbed, of being taken advantage of without even realizing and so on.

But perhaps your parents get too worked up about embarrassment in particular. Because even if you do end up sharing stuff online that you later regret, you still said, 'I want people to see this' before doing so. And that can make all the difference. It means it's less likely to be as 'embarrassing' as your parents fear it could be.

Your parents have never had the experience of being a teenager while having a constant digital audience. It was never part of their thinking. But it is for you.

Hopefully, this will be a good thing.

But it won't always be . . .

'JUST KEEP THAT TO YOURSELF!'

We've looked at a lot of ways that your phone affects you, good and bad. But the important word here is '*your*'. We've focused entirely on how things affect *you*. In fairness, that's what this book is about.

But often, what you get up to on your phone doesn't just affect you, but other people too. People who have no business or interest in being part of your antics, but who get sucked in anyway.

And thanks to your phone and your online activities, you can sometimes end up hurting people, for real, without realizing.

Or without **caring.**

'HOW COULD I HURT OTHER PEOPLE WITH MY PHONE?'

To clarify, I don't mean you literally injure people with your phone. That's actually pretty hard to do, unless you twang it at their skull, like a strangely shaped frisbee?[129]

But you can easily upset them, stress them out or worse.

And I'm not saying you'd ever *deliberately* do this. But unless you live alone in a shack up a mountain, there will always be loads of people in the world around you. That applies to the real world and the digital one. But at least in the digital world everyone *chose* to be there. Nobody's ever accidentally joined TikTok after slipping on a bar of soap.

But many people also choose *not* to be part of the digital, online world. Or only get involved with the parts of it that suit them. Which is fine. But if you take that choice *away* from them and involve them in your phone-based antics without their permission or their awareness, that can be a problem. And it's much easier to do than you think.

---

129. Just to be clear, do *not* attempt this at home. At the very least, you'll wreck your phone.

'I DON'T INVOLVE ANYONE ELSE IN MY ONLINE ACTIVITIES, THOUGH.'

Not on purpose, sure.

But think about, for example, when you hang out with your friends in a public space, such as an amusement park or concert or shopping centre. When you do this, do you also take photos with your phone and share them online?

'USUALLY, YES.'

And are there other people around you too? Strangers, I mean, going about their business?

'IT'S A PUBLIC PLACE, SO YES.'

Right. And do any of them end up in your photos or videos?

'YEAH . . .'

And did you ask those people whether or not they were OK with you posting a photo of them online?

'WELL . . . NO. BUT IT'S JUST ME AND MY FRIENDS! WHO'S GOING TO SEE IT? AND THEY'RE JUST PEOPLE IN THE BACKGROUND; YOU CAN BARELY RECOGNIZE THEM!'

Look, you're probably right. 99.9999 per cent of the time this will do no harm to anyone. They might be well up for it, especially if they're doing something that deliberately draws attention to themselves, like being part of a flashmob. A lot of people actively *want* to be seen by as many people as possible these days and you're technically helping them out.

But often someone might not want to be seen. But they end up in your pictures anyway. Meaning you shared another person's personal details[130] with the digital world without asking. **And that's what I'm getting at:** you had a choice between sharing something with your online friends and followers for their entertainment *or* respecting other people's rights, because it should be their decision whether their details are shared with strangers. You chose the first thing.

You might say you didn't even realize it *was* a choice. Fair enough. **But it shows something very telling:**

We can get so absorbed by our phones and our digital lives that **we intrude into other people's lives and we don't even notice it.**

Again, this *doesn't* make you a bad person. It's incredibly common behaviour these days. Our online interactions and activities often convince us that they are *more* important than strangers in the real world.

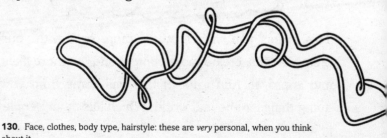

130. Face, clothes, body type, hairstyle: these are *very* personal, when you think about it.

'DIDN'T YOU SAY EARLIER THAT OUR BRAIN FINDS FACE-TO-FACE INTERACTIONS MORE SIGNIFICANT THAN SCREEN ONES?'

I did. And I stand by it. But you're not really interacting with strangers. That's why they're strangers. They're just . . . there.

Your online friends and community, though? *They* interact. They give you 'likes' and laughing emoji reactions, leave positive comments on your pics, send you fun messages, all that. So it's hardly surprising that your interaction-loving brain ends up thinking:

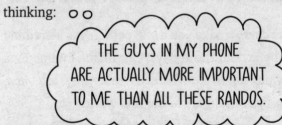

THE GUYS IN MY PHONE ARE ACTUALLY MORE IMPORTANT TO ME THAN ALL THESE RANDOS.

This makes you want to share more stuff with your online friends, create more content and get more likes and approval. And a lot of that will come from you doing things in the real world. Which has other people in it.

Say you're out one day and see someone who you think is wearing funny or embarrassing clothes, or who you think has way too much make-up on or whatever. So you take a sneaky picture and share it with your friends and followers.

Basically, your brain has decided that the amusement and enjoyment of your online friends and community is more important than a stranger's privacy and dignity. Which isn't nice.

'BUT IF THEY DON'T KNOW IT'S HAPPENING, HOW CAN IT HARM THEM?'

Maybe they don't know it's happening, but . . . can you guarantee they *never* will?

The photo you took – anyone in your network could share it somewhere else online. Then it could get passed on further and further, until one day the person in the photograph reads one of those 'Top 30 hideous outfits caught on camera' articles and sees themselves being laughed at by thousands of online strangers.

Ouch.

Of course you didn't *mean* that to happen. Your online friends probably didn't either. It's just an unfortunate result of how the digital world works if you don't pay enough attention.

However, sometimes people take it further and end up disrupting people's actual lives for the sake of their own digital one.

Our old friends; influencers. They regularly get flak for this. Rightly so, in many cases.

Influencers often like to take photos in eye-catching locations. These locations are usually public. Which means there tend to be many other people there too.

For example, there have been many reports of restaurants not being able to serve people quickly enough and staff being busier because so many influencers (and other online types) take ages getting the perfect snaps of their food, drag serving staff in to take photos of them and so on.

When you consider restaurants often live or die depending on how many people they can serve as quickly as possible, this sort of thing is genuinely harmful to others.

Sometimes these digital divas push it further, asking, or *demanding*, that others don't get in the way of their camera, even if they're genuinely holding up or disrupting things around them.

Not too long ago, there was a young woman online complaining about people wandering into her photo because she was trying to take it at a London underground station during the work rush hour. A more cramped, bustling place would be hard to imagine, but she seemed to expect one of the world's busiest cities to just stop – for her photos.

That's an extreme example, but people who spend much of their life online often end up doing this. They believe their content, and entertaining their followers, is far more important than consideration for other people.

'SOME INFLUENCERS DO HAVE *A LOT* OF FOLLOWERS, THOUGH.'

Indeed. Sometimes millions. And if millions of people like someone and want to see what they do, you probably can't blame them for thinking:

I *MUST* BE IMPORTANT!

But this thinking has its own issues.

It's basically become a stereotype of influencers[131] – something we just all sort of assume they do. They'll message a business, shop, artist and say, 'If you give me free stuff, I'll tell my followers about it and they'll buy things from you.' And they present it like they're doing the shop or business a big favour.

The people on the receiving end of this request? They don't like it. They often get angry. Why? Because it's been shown repeatedly that they get basically nothing out of the 'deal'. No increase in business, no more products sold. They just lose out on the money they'd have otherwise got from selling the freebies, like they usually would.

131. Or *wannabe* influencers. Which can very different.

So when influencer types approach people with these requests, it's basically seen as a complete stranger saying,

> YOU KNOW THAT THING YOU DO/MAKE TO EARN MONEY THAT YOU NEED TO SURVIVE? I WANT IT FOR FREE. IN RETURN, YOU'LL GET SOMETHING BASICALLY WORTHLESS.

When you put it like that, it's not exactly tempting. It's flat-out rude.

'WHY DOESN'T IT WORK, THOUGH? YOU SAID INFLUENCERS *DO* INFLUENCE PEOPLE.'

True. But this is another difference between the real and digital worlds.

Imagine having 10,000 followers in the real world. You're basically the head of an army! And a lot of people would respect you. Or fear you. One of the two.

But 10,000 *online* followers? That will be great *for you*. But the person stood next to you in the gym, grumbling because you won't move until you finish recording your video? They don't care at all about your follower count. It doesn't affect them. It's just numbers on a screen. Not even *their* screen.

And the influencer-sorts with big followings who try to use that to get free stuff? They forget something:

Following someone online is *easy*. **And *free*.**

There's a big difference between just looking at someone you like on your phone and actually going out and buying things because that someone told you to. The second thing requires *considerably* more effort and investment (of time *and* money). Which means that, unless you're *very* popular, with *loads* of dedicated followers, telling your online community 'You should buy this thing!' won't do much.

So you end up causing more headaches for other people in the real world because your digital community makes you think that's OK.

'OK, BUT THIS IS MOSTLY ANNOYING, INCONVENIENT STUFF. DOES IT ACTUALLY *HARM* ANYONE?'

Fair enough. What I've mentioned so far is mostly examples of how caring more about the online world can make people less considerate and respectful of real-world people.

But it can definitely be much worse.

For example, plenty of YouTubers and similar rely on pranks for their content, which range from the mild to the extreme. From simply jumping out and startling people, to *apparently* destroying their valuable stuff, to fake proposals, to pretend kidnappings.

Cards on the table, I'm probably biased here because I *hate* pranks. Pranks only work if there's a *victim*. And if you can't be funny without a victim, then you're not funny at all.[132] So if you're constantly pulling pranks, even if it's for your online 'channel', you're essentially

---

132. I'll make an exception if the other person is in on it or enjoys it. But *not* if they only laugh after it happens. There's every chance they're just putting a brave face on it, to lessen the humiliation.

humiliating others and making their life more unpleasant, even if just briefly.

Then there's the spreading of rumours and accusations over group chats and messenger apps. I made it seem silly with Jimmy Gibberish's toilet paper incident, but this can actually be very dangerous.

For example, I'll bet you and your friends have said some things to each other that you'd *never* want anyone else to hear, right? About other people?

'. . . SOMETIMES, YES.'

It's OK. We all do it.

And it wouldn't be unusual to end up sharing some of these darker thoughts over your phone too. But as we now know, sometimes messages can get away from you. Someone could accidentally forward it or could see your screen over your shoulder.

It means some of the things you say privately about others **don't stay private.**

And if someone who *isn't* one of your friends sees the message, they may not see it as a joke. Or know that you didn't mean any harm, that you were just venting. And that can be *very* bad. And remember, this can happen very quickly now that everyone has a phone.

You might *think* it's just a joke or a way to get some justice to take someone down a peg. But it can be like pouring rat poison in someone's tea because they annoy you: they might not die, but it can do them *serious* damage. Making up serious online accusations about someone can be the emotional equivalent of poisoning their tea. Just because you're frustrated.

So yeah, caring more about the people in your phone than the ones you meet in real life *can* be genuinely harmful.

'RIGHT. SO WHAT DO WE DO ABOUT THAT?'

Well, one of the most obvious things to do is to avoid talking to people *entirely* through your phone. I know it's easy and convenient,[133] but it also makes it more likely that your brain ends up thinking:

> THE PEOPLE IN MY PHONE MAKE ME HAPPY, THE ONES OUTSIDE MY PHONE I FEEL NOTHING ABOUT. SO ONLY MY PHONE FRIENDS MATTER.

And maybe just reading this whole thing will have helped? If it means you stop and think, even for a second, before involving actual people, particularly strangers, in your phone activities – that's a good thing. Like, before you take and share that picture or pull that prank, quickly ask yourself,

> WOULD I BE *OK* WITH IT IF THIS WAS DONE TO *ME*?

---

133. It may also not be an option if you're too socially anxious or neurodivergent.

The answer might be 'Yes', because you love sharing your antics online. And the person you're doing it to could feel the exact opposite, which is still a problem. But at least you've *thought* about them and what they might like or not like. And that's an important step.

And, of course, there's always your parents. They can help remind you to consider other people's needs and rights. They spend enough time thinking about yours, after all.

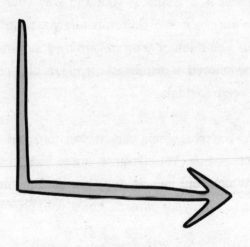

'YOU NEED TO KEEP PARENTAL CONTROLS ON'

We've looked at so many different things about your phone and how it affects you, and why your parents tend to worry about it. Unfortunately, you're still young. So what you think or want, regarding your phone, can often be ignored or dismissed. Or so lots of parents and adults seem to think.

If you're a typical young person, you don't just sit there and accept that. You disagree, argue your case, push back. Which your parents don't like. And so you argue. Regularly. With your parents. About your phone.

That's the whole point of this book: to understand these arguments and why they happen. And maybe even to win them now and again. Parents are stubborn, but stranger things have happened.

Although, this leads to one last relevant question: who's actually in charge of what happens with your phone? Who should get the final say in what you do with it? You or your parents?

'THAT'S EASY. IT'S ME. YOU JUST SAID IT'S *MY* PHONE.'

I did. And you have a point.

It's got all *your* accounts and settings and pictures and apps on it.

All the contacts saved on it are *your* friends and family.

The alerts or notification are meant for *you*.

It may even be in a phone case *you* chose.

So yeah, everything about your phone basically has your name on it, so who else should have the final say in what's done with it?

'EXACTLY!'

One question, though: who *paid* for it?

If you're like most young people, your parents paid for it. And if your phone is on a monthly tariff, your parents are *still* paying for it.

It may be your phone in most ways, but that's only possible because your parents are willing to cover the costs of it. And many parents feel this ultimately gives them a say in what happens with it. Maybe the final say.

Would you say they have a point?

'WELL, YES . . . BUT NO . . . MAYBE?'

Yeah, it's a tricky one.

Some feel it's simple: if you paid for it, you own it, so you're in charge of it. Like if someone owns a house that someone else lives in, it may be that person's *home*, but the owner could still kick them out if they wanted. Because it belongs to them.

Renting out a house is a very different situation to buying something *for* someone. If your parents bought their friends an expensive bottle of wine, could they turn around three years later and demand to have it back? Pretty much everyone would consider that ridiculous.

That's especially true with your parents and you. They're supposed to pay for your things! That's, like, part of the deal of being parents. Parents are *expected* to support their children and that includes financially.[134]

It's not 100 per cent clear how phones fit in, though. Your parents having to pay for your things usually means paying for *essentials*. Things you genuinely need for day-to-day life, like somewhere to sleep, a place to live, food, clothes, etc.

Do you *need* a phone? Surely that's a *luxury*, like designer clothes or video games? Something you don't need but *want*. And giving your child everything they want, no matter what? Like I say, we've all met kids who've been raised like that. They're not the best.

---

134. If you do have the sort of parents who think 'I paid for it, so it belongs to me' applies to their own children's stuff, ask when they paid your grandparents back for everything they spent on them.

So it's up to your parents whether they want to fork out for a phone for you.[135] If they do, it might be with the condition that they have the last word on what you do with it. And if you want the phone, you've got to suck it up.

Only . . . *is* a phone really a luxury, in this day and age? Think of all the things you *couldn't* do without one, all the social and schooling stuff you'd miss out on. Many would consider phones essential now.

And sometimes parents can trip themselves up by constantly telling you that phones are bad and that you shouldn't want or need one, but *also* regularly insisting you keep your phone with you, like when you're outdoors without them or in school. Even if your teachers are telling you the opposite.

Basically, your parents say your phone is bad for you, dangerous *and* keeps you safe. Could anyone blame you for being confused about where they're coming from?

135. This is assuming they can afford one but don't want to. If they *can't* afford one, because phones aren't cheap and times are hard, that's a whole different matter.

'ARE PHONES DANGEROUS? I THOUGHT YOU SAID THEY WEREN'T?'

Well, not quite. It's more that they are unlikely to be as damaging or harmful as many parents seem to think. I mean, given how many people have phones now, you'd think if they did do serious harm, we'd have noticed already.

But that doesn't mean they *definitely* don't do anything bad. Because they can do, as we saw in Chapter 1. But then, pretty much everything you enjoy is 'bad for you' to some extent if you have too much of it.

Do phones regularly do serious, lasting damage? We're still looking into that. And that uncertainty is annoying.

If phones *can* cause lasting harm, **your parents have a *responsibility* to keep some sort of control over yours.**

Like, if you're a child playing with a foam hammer, you can be left alone to get on with it. But if you're using, say, a kitchen knife, perhaps when learning how to cook, your parents need to be more 'hands-on' and actually be there to supervise you, to make sure you don't hurt yourself. They could get in serious trouble if they didn't do this.

Remember Stirling Moss being given a car when he was nine years old? If your parents did that for you *now*, the authorities would get involved.

Basically, the more dangerous phones are thought to be, the more control parents will want over yours. For your safety and their peace of mind.

However, as we've seen many times, your parents often don't see phones the same way you do and this can mean they go too far or get too heavy-handed.

For example, ever been in the middle of an interesting group chat with your friends, only for your parents to suddenly insist you put your phone away *right now*, because you've been on it for too long? With no concern for what you were doing on it or how suddenly cutting you off might affect you?

It happens a lot. No doubt your parents think they're

doing a good, helpful thing. But imagine
if you were chilling with your friends
outdoors, just hanging out like you do,
and suddenly your car pulled up and your
parents jumped out, grabbed you, bundled you
into the back seat and sped away.

That would be a massively uncool thing to do. But that's
pretty much what's happening, just in the virtual sense,
when they cut you off from your phone while you're in
the middle of engaging with others.

Thcy just don't see it that way.

'BUT WHAT CAN I DO ABOUT IT? I DON'T CONTROL MY PARENTS.'

Yeah, it's tricky. The whole 'my house, my rules' thing
still applies at the end of the day. So between that, their
age and their ability to pay for things, your parents will
probably always be the ones making the final decisions
– about your phone or anything else. Not much to be
done about that, usually.

The issue is that, while their intentions are normally good, parents can get carried away by focusing on things they *can* control and overlooking things they *can't*.

Parents can't control everything you do with your phone, **but they *can* control how and when you use it**. And as a result, they'll often feel like they ***should.***

In many ways, this is fair. Reasonable, even. It's your parents' job to look out for you, to keep you safe. They may go over the top with this at times, sure, but their hearts are still in the right place. Technically.

And as much as I'm sure you'll not want to hear this, there are *plenty* of times when your parents genuinely do know better. You're still young, still developing and learning, while your parents have been around the block a few times. And just like how you'd be constantly nervous about a five-year-old cousin handling your phone, parents will always be a bit anxious about you having unchecked access to yours.

On the other hand,
your parents' decisions
and instructions about
your phone won't always
be totally sensible. Parents are *constantly*
being told that your phone is doing you harm
– by other overprotective parents and adults with a
suspicion of new technology that everyone seems to
end up with as they age.

But this can mean they're blinded to just how important
and vital phones have become in the modern world.
Particularly for young people like yourself, who are still
figuring out who they are and how the world works,
something phones can be *very* helpful with.

The end result of this is that your parents will constantly
be thinking about the risks and harmful consequences
of you using your phone too much and wanting to do
something about it, but never consider the harmful
consequences of taking it *from* you.

Maybe you can now start a discussion with
your parents about this. They have their
useful perspectives to offer, but you
have yours too. Let them know

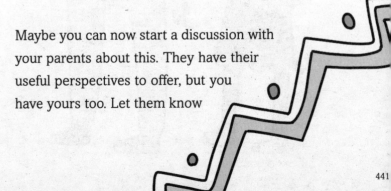

what it is you're *truly* doing with your phone, and how both it and their involvement in you using it affects you. Give your parents the information they need that they presumably don't have.

You should be able to do that now. After all, you've just finished a book all about it.

SOME FINAL THOUGHTS

Phones have been one of the biggest game-changers ever seen. And they can do, and affect, so much. We've seen how phones impact your health, memory, truth, education, friendships, relationships, beliefs, privacy, money, business, identity and loads more.

Add to this the fact that you and your parents have *very* different experiences and attitudes towards them, which mix things up even more, and it's no wonder you and they disagree about your phone so much. There's just so much to not agree about!

That's also why there are no easy answers or simple instructions for how to solve all that. At least none that I've found. And I've been looking harder than most.

It's just too complex and probably requires constant back and forth between you and your parents. Sometimes you'll need to test boundaries, like not letting your parents be involved with what you're doing with your phone, despite their protests. Sometimes it'll be negotiating limits, like agreeing a certain amount of screen time and sticking to it without them having to nag you. Sometimes you'll need to earn and return trust, like your parents allowing you to go and stay out more, as long as you keep in touch and let them know where you are. With your phone. And more stuff like that.

When there's no easy answer, you often have to make do **with loads of smaller, more complex ones.**

But in a way that's helpful. Whether you're hitting your teens or are well into them, evidence suggests that that's what this age is all about. You're growing, maturing, to eventually become an independent adult. Which means leaving your childhood behind.

And a big part of that is becoming independent of your parents and figuring out the relationship between you all over again, to get to one where you're more like equals. But picking apart and rebuilding, piece by piece and step by step, something as powerful as the relationship between parent and child? That's a delicate, stressful, emotional process. Which is why parents and teens have been arguing for as long as parents and teens have existed.

As we've seen, phones have complicated this even more. They let influential strangers with murky intentions into your life. They make an even bigger mess of your sleep. They add more issues about money and expense into your relationships. They blur the lines between parents, teachers, home and school. And more besides.

But, on the other hand, they may also provide something useful. Something for both you and your parents to zero in on and work out your differences around. Without things getting too personal. Here's hoping, anyway.

And if you and your parents aren't seeing eye-to-eye on things, your phone can be a big help. Because, despite their best efforts, your parents don't know everything. And even if they *do* know stuff, it's often harder to talk to them about more 'sensitive' matters. Your phone can be very useful here.

- It allows you to find vital information from the safety of your room.

- It connects you with sympathetic others with helpful experiences and expertise.

- It allows you to express yourself safely, and with more control and security, and to a bigger community, than any young person in history.

All this means you need to be careful with it too, of course. And maybe that's something else your parents can help with. They've seen more of the world; they may have better luck telling the good from the bad when it comes to what you encounter online with your phone.

You're on your way to becoming your own person, looking to make a difference in the world, both real and digital. I can't tell you how to do that, although I like to think I've provided some insight, some tools to help you on your way.

At the end of the day, though, it's all up to you to figure out your own path.

Good luck!

ACKNOWLEDGEMENTS

You know, it takes a lot more than one person to write a book. In many ways, I'm just the guy who presses the buttons on the laptop keyboard. And yes, I do still do all my work on a laptop. I'm old, remember. But anyway, although it's my name on the cover, this book wouldn't exist if it weren't for the following people.

- My wife, Vanita, for keeping everything else in our life going while I worked on this.

- My children, Millen and Kavita, for showing me just how great young people are and why they deserve to be respected.

- My mother Sian and my late father Peter, for being the sort of parents that I could write a whole book about why parents are rubbish and they don't mind in the slightest.

- Kelly Bubbins and the students of Willows High School, and Caroline Guest and the students of Monmouthshire Comprehensive

School, for letting me visit and explaining a *lot* of things to me.

- Finally, my editor Tom, who was *very* patient with me and my multiple failures to stick to deadlines.

RESOURCES

While I hope the information provided in this book has been useful, you may well be one of those less fortunate young people dealing with more serious issues, whether it's concerning your mental health, relationships or other important matters.

If this does describe you, here are resources you may find helpful.

CHILDLINE

www.childline.org.uk

A free, private and confidential service for young people under the age of 19, where you can talk about anything, whatever your worry, whenever you need help.

FIND A HELPLINE

www.findahelpline.com

Helplines (also known as hotlines or crisis lines) provide immediate crisis counselling, emotional support and information – for free. This is the most accurate helpline resource in the world. They hold relationships with crisis centres in over 130 countries.

HEALTH FOR TEENS

www.healthforteens.co.uk

An online resource created by the NHS to deliver guidance and support for struggling young people aged 11–19. They cover concerns from physical, mental and sexual health to societal pressures and lifestyle changes. They also run a ChatHealth service where young people are able to contact their local public health nursing team 24/7 via text message. Go to www.healthforteens.co.uk/health/about-chathealth for more information about the ChatHealth texting service in your local area.

KOOTH

www.kooth.com

A judgement-free forum to get advice, help others and share your story.

MIND

www.mind.org.uk

A mental health charity that aims to empower anyone experiencing a mental health problem by providing advice and support, to make sure that no one has to face these problems alone.

PAPYRUS

www.papyrus-uk.org

The national charity working to give hope to young people under the age of 35 and to prevent young suicide. They provide confidential support and advice to vulnerable young people or those concerned about their loved ones.

YOUNG MINDS

www.youngminds.org.uk

A leading charity that fights for children and young people's mental health. They offer information and guidance to enlighten and support those suffering from mental health issues.

INDEX